The
SACRIFICE
of the
MASSES

Robert M. Hoatson, Ph.D.

Copyright © 2025
Robert M. Hoatson, Ph.D. or
Diamond Publishing Co.

All rights reserved.
Published by Diamond Publishing Co.

The events, places, and conversations in this memoir have been recreated from Dr. Hoatson's memory and to the best of his ability. When necessary, the names and identifying characteristics of individuals and places have been changed to maintain anonymity. The publisher assumes no risk.

No part of this document may be reproduced or transmitted in any form or by any means, electronic, mechanical, photocopying, recording, or otherwise, without prior written permission by either Robert M. Hoatson, Ph.D. or Diamond Publishing Co.

For information regarding permission, write to:

Robert M. Hoatson, Ph.D.
c/o Road-to-Recovery
P.O. Box 279
Livingston, NJ 07039

or Contact
www.Road-to-Recovery.org
or
Diamond Publishing
DiamondPublishing@yahoo.com

ISBN: 978-1-955794-10-7
First Edition, 2025

Printed in the U.S.A.

Robert M. Hoatson, Ph.D.

TABLE OF CONTENTS

Praise for The Sacrifice of the Masses vii
DEDICATION AND TRIBUTE xi
INTRODUCTION. xv
PART I xxi
BOBBY AND SEAN 1
SEAN AND JOEY 15
BOBBY, SEAN, AND VINCE. 23
IT WAS MY TURN TO COME FORWARD 29
MY ONE-YEAR NOVITIATE- BOTH YEARS 33
MY SCHOLASTICATE YEAR BROUGHT MORE ABUSE. 39
A NEW SUPERIOR. 43
FORE! AND FOREPLAY 49
MY NON-PROFIT AND TROUBLE WITH ARCHBISHOP JOHN J. MYERS . . 55
ONE PEDO MOVING IN, ME MOVING OUT. 59
SENATE HEARING TESTIMONY AND MY SUBSEQUENT FIRING. 63
ASSISTING VICTIMS AND HELPING MYSELF HEAL 71
MY LAWSUIT AND SUBSEQUENT SUSPENSION. 79
THE MIRACLE STORY OF ASSISTING A VICTIM 85
ROAD TO RECOVERY'S HUMBLE BEGINNINGS. 93
JIMMY CRAIG HOATSON, MY FIRST COUSIN 99
PART II 105
AN INSIDER'S EXPERIENCE 107
MY ORDINATION 113
MY FIRST PRIESTLY TRANSFER 125
BUS ACCIDENT 141
NO PLACE TO GO 151
SEXUAL ABUSE'S HIDDEN ISSUES. 157
MY FATHER HAS A STROKE 165
FRONT PAGE NEWS 167
REPRESSED MEMORY COMES FLOODING BACK. 171
ANXIETY SETS IN, I SEEK HELP 175
OFFICE POLITICS 181
EDUCATOR OF THE YEAR. 189
EVEN IN ELEMENTARY SCHOOL 195
FROM SUICIDAL VICTIM TO SURVIVOR 203
MURDER, HE WROTE 207
LEAVING THE PRIESTHOOD AND BLOWING THE WHISTLE – AGAIN . . 213
FREEDOM FROM THE MAFIA. 217
I KEPT MY PROMISE, AND JESUS KEPT HIS. 219
HEROES GOVERNOR FRANK KEATING AND 227
ATTORNEY MITCHELL GARABEDIAN 227
WHAT IS WRONG WITH THIS PICTURE?. 233
PHOTOS 235

Praise for The Sacrifice of the Masses

"Bob Hoatson tells a heroic story. Here is a man who has dedicated his life to helping other survivors of sexual abuse and to calling out institutional evil despite the personal cost. Painful, riveting, and essential reading for anyone who cares about justice and truth."

Carole Garibaldi Rogers
Author and Director, Voice of the Faithful, New Jersey

"Reader BEWARE! This is a very vivid and detailed book for which you will want to be prepared. It is an honest, painful, extremely descriptive, and yet very necessary account of the current and past sexual abuse atrocities in the Roman Catholic Church. As a fellow survivor, it captured so well all that we manage every day and all that we have experienced. This is a painful and very important reading for all of us today."

Gerard J. McGlone, SJ, PhD
Senior Research Fellow
Berkley Center for Religion, Peace, and World Affairs
Georgetown University
Washington, D.C. 20007

Robert M. Hoatson, Ph.D.

"The Sacrifice of the Masses promises to be a blockbuster when it is released on the U.S. publishing scene in 2025 and for good reasons.

The 'Sacrifice of the Masses' is the novelised autobiography of (Dr) Robert Hoatson, a towering figure on the U.S. East Coast as a supremely gifted educator in his younger maturity and, over the last twenty years, one of the pioneer supporters of those men and women abused sexually by priests or Brothers in the Catholic Church.

In 1994, Robert left the Irish Christian Brothers to pursue ordination to the Roman Catholic priesthood. He was ordained a priest in 1997 and served at parishes throughout northern New Jersey and was also Principal of Holy Trinity School in Hackensack and Director of Schools at Our Lady of Good Counsel Parish in Newark.

However, Fr. Robert was already involved in assisting victims of abuse in the Church and this is THE major focus of The Sacrifice of the Masses."

Brother/Dr. Barry M Coldrey
Edmund Rice Christian Brothers
Victoria, AUSTRALIA

"For centuries, the Catholic Church has been considered the strongest moral voice on the international scene. In a scathing personal analysis of the Church's institutional abuse of power, Dr. Robert Hoatson recounts stories that are colloquial, painful to hear, and confessional in *The Sacrifice of the Masses*, as he reveals the dark side of this religious institution, capturing in disturbing detail not only his own journey and the journeys of many other survivors of sexual abuse, but also the road to healing and recovery. With sharp words of reproach, he criticizes this religious institution to which he had dedicated four decades of his life, as a religious brother and then priest, for allowing the clergy abuse, especially of children and teenagers, to spread like a cancer throughout society. He views this as a lethal cancer that has destroyed thousands of lives physically and emotionally over the decades, labeling this sickness as "soul murder," equivalent to a genocide. Throughout the tragic narratives of survivors he has met over many years, all of whom abused by clergy, Robert Hoatson laments this "soul murder" and calls on the Church to accept accountability and commit to reform, while addressing a most profound, still unanswered question: Is it still possible for this institution to redeem itself?"

Susan A. Michalczyk, Ph.D.
John J. Michalczyk, Ph.D.
Documentary Co-Producers:
Who Takes Away the Sins: Witnesses to Clergy Abuse
A Matter of Conscience: Confronting Clergy Abuse

Robert M. Hoatson, Ph.D.

DEDICATION AND TRIBUTE

This book is dedicated to my loving family and the thousands of sexual abuse victim/survivors, especially my deceased first cousin, James Craig Hoatson, and advocates who have edified and supported me through the decades of my own recovery from multiple acts of sexual abuse. I was sexually abused from ages three to thirty, including religious men and clergy members, and were it not for outstanding mental health professionals such as J. A. Loftus, SJ, (RIP), A. Ronald Sorvino (RIP), William T. Richardson (RIP), Benedict Vicarisi, and miracle medications that have been created to help the brain heal, relax, and function adequately, I would not be where I am today.

Besides the talents of medical health professionals, I have been fortunate to have had outstanding legal representation by Attorney Mitchell Garabedian of Boston since 2003. Attorney Garabedian is the preeminent clergy sexual abuse attorney in the country, as demonstrated by the 2016 Academy Award-winning Best Picture, "Spotlight," in which he was portrayed by actor Stanley Tucci. Attorney Garabedian continues to represent me well.

My parents, Archie and Pat Hoatson, are resting peacefully in the Kingdom promised them, and they raised five children to be moral, ethical, and honest. My siblings and their spouses, Bill and Grace Hoatson; Richard and Maureen Hoatson; Thomas and Lynn Oliver-Hoatson; and Patricia McCormick have walked with me since age three to the present to attempt to understand "what's up with me" and the after-effects of sexual abuse in general. Their children have been fabulous as well.

I am grateful to my co-founder and President of Road to Recovery, Inc., Msgr. Kenneth E. Lasch, whom you will read about extensively in this manuscript, and the Board of Directors and Board of Advisors of Road to Recovery, Inc. What Msgr. Lasch endured from *his fellow clerics and bishops as a whistleblower and advocate was nothing short of torture. Road to Recovery, Inc. has assisted over five thousand victims and their families since 2003. Special thanks to Anthony W. Vasile, CPA, and Michele Fronduto, CPA, of Vasile and Fronduto, LLP, and Ernest Barbato who have been our pro-bono accountants and bookkeeper since the very beginning in 2003. Their reward in heaven will be great.*

Thanks, too, to my colleagues in the Catholic Whistleblowers organization. Each one of us suffered as a result of telling the truth. The late Sr. Maureen Paul Turlish, SND de N. (RIP) and Fr. Gary Hayes (RIP) are memorialized as heroes in their dogged pursuit of justice for all sexual abuse victim/survivors. The rest of the Coordinating Committee of Catholic Whistleblowers has held the Church's feet to the fire in many areas of clergy sexual abuse: Rev. John P. Bambrick; Sr. Sally Butler, OP (RIP); Rev. Patrick Collins, Rev. James Connell; Rev. Thomas Doyle, OP; Rev. Msgr. Kenneth Lasch; Rev. Ronald Lemmert; Helen Rainforth, Sr. Claire Smith, OSU (RIP); Rev. Bruce Teague; Susan Vance; Patrick Wall; Rev. Mark White, and myself.

I am edified by and grateful to Terry McKiernan and Anne Barrett Doyle of BishopAccountability.org for compiling, on a global basis, a library of documents and evidence regarding clergy sexual abuse. And to my generous and compassionate colleagues in the Voice of the Faithful New Jersey, I say, thank you so much.

Working with my publisher, Diamond Publishing, and its leader, Katy Collins, has been one of the finest experiences of my life. No task was too cumbersome, no problem too serious, and no discussion ever too honest and transparent. Editor Bridget Fuchsel's keen eye and superior knowledge and grasp of the English language surpassed my expectations.

Finally, to all my students and colleagues at St. Cecilia's School, East Harlem; Blessed Sacrament High School, New Rochelle, New

York, and one of the finest persons and educator/coaches I ever met, Harry Hart (RIP); Rice High School, Harlem, New York; Catholic Memorial High School, Boston, MA, especially my former freshman homeroom student D.C., a courageous victim/survivor with whom I stay in contact; Fordham University; William H. Sadlier Publishing Co., especially my close friend and colleague, the late John Stack, who still keeps me laughing; St. John's University, New York, and my colleague in the School of Education, Dean Geraldine Chapey (RIP); Sacred Heart High and Elementary Schools, Yonkers, New York, and some of the finest educators and staff I have ever worked with: Helen Nevin, Associate Principal; Kieran Stack, Assistant Principal; Jean Borelli, my secretary; and Sr. Helen Fleming, SC, (RIP), a master teacher of French.

I also am grateful to the parishioners and colleagues of St. Margaret of Cortona Parish, Little Ferry, NJ; St. Andrew's Parish, Bayonne, NJ; Holy Trinity Parish and School, Hackensack, NJ, especially my top-notch secretary, Connie Malagiere; Our Lady of Good Counsel Schools, Newark, NJ, with superior Elementary School Principal Pat McGrath; Our Lady of Lourdes, West Orange, NJ; St. Mary's Parish, Closter, NJ, St. Catharine's Parish, Glen Rock, NJ; and Nativity Parish, Midland Park, NJ. – Thanks for your love and support.

Finally, to my very best priest friend, mentor, and fellow victim/survivor of clergy sexual abuse, Fr. Philip F. Fabiano, OFM, Cap.
– REST IN PEACE, PHILIP

Robert M. Hoatson, Ph.D.

INTRODUCTION

With great sadness, I begin this book with a necessary judgment. The Roman Catholic Church is the most corrupt organization in the world, and it has been for centuries. I refer not to Catholics who, for the most part, try each day to live the Christian faith. I refer to the institution of the Roman Catholic Church, its leadership, its supervisors, and its so-called "hierarchs." Popes, Cardinals, Archbishops, and Bishops have been and are as immoral, unethical, dishonest, untruthful, and unscrupulous as any group of so-called leaders in the history of the world, and their ranks are getting worse.

The Holocaust was no doubt the most depraved and perverted scandal in modern history, leading to the extinction of six million Jews and the rise of autocracy and dictatorship. The African slave trade was another example of depravity and deviance, leading to the destruction of millions of African lives and culminating in the world-wide racism that continues to this day. The reason for these "holocausts" is simple: corrupt leaders who sought unlimited power and used it against fellow brothers and sisters. Numerous outrageous genocides have scarred humanity, and the abuse of human beings continues.

Corruption in the Catholic Church has led to its Holocaust; namely, the whole-scale murder of millions of children's and vulnerable adults' souls through sexual abuse by clergy and other church personnel. And the reason for this Holocaust: corruption among Church leaders and their quest for unbridled power and money that summarily rejected Christianity so they could abuse power. Sexual abuse of children, teenagers, and vulnerable adults is the Roman Catholic Church's Holocaust, just like the German Holocaust murdered Jews, the British Holocaust murdered the Irish, the Sudanese murdered its own, the Ottoman Empire attempted to erase Armenians from the face of the earth, and the Tutsi and Hutu tribal members' murders in Rwanda, to name but a few. Currently, a cor-

rupt Vladamir Putin of Russia is attempting to create a Ukrainian Holocaust.

To this day, the Catholic Church has never acknowledged its soul murder of millions of its members, and it continues to hold on to traditions and policies that guarantee that the Church's holocaust will never end. Unless and until the Church ends its blatant hypocrisy and antiquated ways, no one will be safe in the Church. Most recently, Pope Francis said that gays and those in gay marriages should be treated with kindness and compassion, but a few weeks later endorsed an edict that forbids priests to bless same sex marriages. Pope Francis had then encouraged every citizen of the world to receive the Covid vaccine in order to control the virus, but then many clerics objected to the Johnson and Johnson vaccine because it may contain parts of aborted fetuses. The Catholic Church cannot get out if its way and the only answer is quicker bureaucratic implosion or absolute elimination with a start over. Jesus would approve, I believe.

The Church cannot get its story straight because it has abandoned the example of its founder; Jesus. As one reads and internalizes the work of Jesus during his earthly life, there would never be statements such as, "Homosexuals are disordered" that lasted for centuries in the Church. Keeping divorced and remarried persons away from the Eucharist if they don't get annulments of their marriages is absurd and Jesus would have been the first to say so. Engaging in ridiculous and unimportant items such as whether allergic Catholics can receive gluten-free hosts or whether alcoholic priests and parishioners can partake of grape juice rather than altar wine exposes the fact that the Church is more concerned with what's outside than what's inside, which is objectively in opposition to Jesus' admonition to focus on the inside and not the outside. He urged that all of us clean our "insides" before we pay attention to the "outside." The Church's leadership has fostered the opposite for centuries and refuses to follow the admonitions of Jesus.

One can examine Jesus' words and actions in the Gospels and other Scriptural documents and conclude that the Roman Catholic Church is as far away from his message as Earth is from Mars.

Jesus used parables to teach; the Church hierarchy uses intimidation and legalese not to teach but to keep the faithful in line and obedient. Jesus freed people; the hierarchy of the Church enslaves people. The hierarchy for years claimed that some of God's people, homosexuals, were disordered. Imagine a Christ-based religion calling any of God's creations disordered. And, when it pretends to reverse its opinion on whether homosexuals are disordered, it continues to call homosexual behavior sinful.

In 2021, Pope Francis had implored his followers to accept homosexuals as brothers and sisters in the Lord, but several weeks later, he had agreed with a Vatican Congregation that same sex marriages may not be blessed by Catholic clergy. The line in that document that was particularly insulting and anti-Christian is, "God does not condone sin." Is there any doubt that Jesus would be rolling over in his grave had he not purportedly risen from the dead?

According to some data and my own personal observation, as many as seventy percent of the clergy are gay, and where perhaps the same percentage of the hierarchy are also gay, the anti-gay pronouncements from the largely gay clergy lead me to conclude they are self-hating and guilt and shame-inducing. How can a gay clergyman support the Church's tenets on homosexuality from the pulpit when those very tenets of the Church consider him less than human in many ways? Is there any wonder that the Catholic Church in particular has a problem with sexual abuse? How can a gay clergymen condemn who he himself is? That self-hating behavior can only lead to a dysfunctional psychology and spirituality.

Jesus made it very clear that whoever abuses a child should have a millstone tied around his neck and thrown into the sea. Yet, the

Church and, in particular, its hierarchy, have treated clergy sexual abusers and their enablers with kid gloves, choosing not to treat sexual abuse of minors, teenagers, and vulnerable adults as crimes and their actors as criminals; rather, the hierarchy talks about mercy, forgiveness, and restitution for abusers rather than victims.

Nothing has changed in the Church hierarchy, and nothing can change. Bishops are still selected using antiquated and secretive evaluation forms that end up in the Congregation for Bishops, a committee of Papal appointments, mainly Cardinals, who promulgate the incestuous composition of like-minded clergymen. Lay people, who have called for greater participation in the selection of their bishops, have largely been ignored. Popes, Cardinals, Archbishops, and Bishops select themselves, meaning the hierarchs want rookie bishops who will promulgate the antiquated policies and practices of the past and present. In addition, compromised members of the hierarchs, such as Cardinals Theodore McCarrick and Donald Wuerl, recommend clergymen who act like they do and who will not "rat them out," as in the Mafia. To think that Bishop Donald Wuerl, who resigned as a Cardinal because of his corrupt behavior, was chosen years ago to go to the Archdiocese of Seattle to "spy" on a Christ-like and beloved Archbishop Raymond Hunthausen. The actions of the pope were the epitome of hypocrisy, arrogance, and betrayal.

Jesus spent much of his time on earth railing against the "wolves in sheep's clothing;" namely, leaders of the Jews in his day. Jesus was even criticized by the "political" Pharisees and Scribes for healing on the Sabbath and treating the lowest of the low with empathy and compassion. Jesus hated politics, but the hierarchy of the Catholic Church is one hundred percent behind politics and politicians. Bishops are appointed through political processes, not processes that identify holy, empathetic, and compassionate clergymen. Furthermore, leadership of the Church has been open only to men, even though any Catholic may be appointed a Cardinal. Church leaders have never appointed a woman to a high position in the Church, another outrageous tradition and policy that needs to be changed.

As I was writing this introduction, Pope Francis instituted new policies for Vatican officials which intended to address the financial corruption of high-level Vatican officials, and he was not referring to housekeepers, Swiss Guards, or landscapers. He referred to Popes, Cardinals, Archbishops, Bishops, and probably Monsignors. They are the men whose behaviors have been an embarrassment and scandal to the Church for centuries, not just decades. However, if Pope Francis thought that limiting financial and other gifts that Vatican officials may accept to only cash and items not to exceed forty-eight Euros, he was living in "La La" land. Vatican officials are wealthy, all of them, and reside in grand palazzos. These men have feathered their nests for years in order to live in the lap of luxury.

One needs only to read Jason Berry's book, "Render Unto Rome: The Secret Life of Money in the Catholic Church" to understand the centuries-old pursuit and misuse of money by the Vatican. In dioceses around the world, there isn't a bishop who isn't living a life of ease and comfort, even in the poorest countries of the world. Bishops wont for nothing, and if the donations from parishioners in weekly collections and other fund-raising projects decline, Bishops simply raise the taxes on parishes to make sure the dioceses (and consequently, the Bishops) do not suffer a decrease in their quality of life. It is nothing but scandalous, arrogant, and completely contrary to the spirit of the Gospel. As one of the Catholic Whistleblowers organization, Fr. Patrick Collins, said so well in a movie produced by Drs. Susan and John Michalczyk of Boston College, "The bishops are concerned about two things: their asses and their assets." Another way to say it is that a Bishop is concerned primarily about his image and his wallet. There isn't a bishop in the world who would settle for living a lifestyle less than that of a prince or king. A German bishop, known in the media as the "Bishop of Bling," was removed by Pope Francis in 2014 only after it was revealed that he had spent over 30 million euros on his residence and accoutrements. In the Diocese of Rockville Centre, Long Island, New York, Bishop William Murphy, a disciple of Cardinal Bernard Law, the disgraced

Robert M. Hoatson, Ph.D.

Archbishop of Boston, MA, evicted a group of religious women from a convent on the headquarters' grounds in order that a wine cellar might be built for his meetings with donors and others.

This book is about sexual abuse, of course, but the sexual abuse I describe is based on the abuse of power and authority. Power is abused every moment of every day by Popes, Cardinals, Archbishops, Bishops, Monsignors, Major Superiors of Religious Orders, rank-and-file priests, and nuns. Instead of shepherding in humility and simplicity, these men and women feel entitled, and ordinary Catholics suffer as a result. Their behavior, in general, is anathema to the Gospel.

PART I

Robert M. Hoatson, Ph.D.

CHAPTER ONE

BOBBY AND SEAN

In the Catholic tradition, the Feast of the Epiphany, also known as the Feast of the Three Kings, occurs several days after Christmas. January 6 is the usual day for the Feast, and in East Harlem, where I taught for one year as a Christian Brother, a large parade is held to commemorate the Feast. The Three Kings Feast is an important feast for the Hispanic community (and all Christians) because it ends the twelve days of Christmas. The night before, January 5, is often celebrated as the Night of the Kings and is when family and communal meals, gift-giving to children, and celebrations prepare for the big feast the next day.

"Epiphany" in Greek means "appearance" or "manifestation." The historical Three Kings—Melchior, Caspar, and Balthazar—presented the new-born Jesus with gifts of gold, frankincense, and myrrh, each representing a different aspect of Jesus' Kingship. In the New Testament account, the Three Kings bowed in adoration and recognized that this newborn held even more authority and power than they did.

On the Night of Kings, January 5, 2002, another "epiphany" took place when *Boston Globe* editor Marty Baron gave the go-ahead to print a Sunday edition revealing what would become perhaps the greatest scandal in the history of the Catholic Church. Some thought Marty Baron, a Jew, would be perceived as anti-Catholic and anti-Christian for filling the newsstands with a Sunday newspaper that exposed the clergy abuse scandal in the Commonwealth of Massachusetts on the Feast of the Epiphany. The *Globe's* "Spotlight Team" spent months researching the cover-up of clergy sexual abuse by Catholic leaders such as Cardinal Bernard Law and his predecessors, and January 6 was the culmination of interviews with victim/survivors and their families. They pored through thousands of documents and worked with attorneys who had received hundreds of claims of clergy sexual abuse for decades.

That day, I drove to New York City to obtain a copy of the *Boston Globe* because I couldn't find it anywhere in New Jersey. I sat on Eighth Avenue near Columbus Circle, reading the article in the hard copy. I wanted to see what the actual hard copy looked like because the internet copy was slightly different. I remember drying a tear or two from my eyes as I read for two reasons: I cried sad tears for my fellow victim/survivors and their abuse, and I cried happy tears because finally, we victim/survivors had been heard, found credible, and vindicated. I had spent nearly forty years in service to the Church, and this was my first hope that the truth about the evil and corruption of the hierarchy, where the real problem lay, might be addressed.

The "Spotlight Team" had become instant heroes to victim/survivors, enemies of much of the Boston and national Catholic clergy, and somewhere in between to Catholics of Boston and the rest of the country. One thing was evident: Marty Baron's decision to publish a Sunday newspaper on January 6, 2002, with a blockbuster headline about the Catholic Church got the attention it deserved. Who would have thought it would take another Jew (like Jesus) to hold arrogant and corrupt church personnel accountable for their crimes and misdeeds?

When I arrived at my ministry site on January 7, 2002, as the Director of Schools of Our Lady of Good Counsel Parish, City of Newark, I greeted the elementary and high school children that morning with extra love and happiness. Some of the staff had seen the article, too, and they spent a few minutes discussing the basics with me before the school bell rang. Most were happy for me since they knew I had been fighting on behalf of clergy sexual abuse victims for some time, but most had no idea of the depth of my personal story.

The *Boston Globe* article gave me courage and energy. I had never revealed my story of sexual abuse in the Christian Brothers to more than two or three persons, and those persons never helped me take my story to those with authority or leadership. They never mentioned my abuse again, and I was disappointed. After the *Boston Globe's* revelations, I began to follow daily all the stories written about clergy sexual abuse. A website called "Abuse Tracker," sponsored by an archival organization that preserved information about clergy sexual abuse, began to publish all the stories written internationally about clergy sexual abuse. I was glued to the computer because I knew the clergy abuse crisis was horrific, and reading more and more about cases around the world gave me hope that things would soon change. They did and didn't.

A few months after the *Globe* article appeared, I was sitting in my office at Our Lady of Good Counsel when the phone rang. "Father Bob," the woman said, "It's Millie Hudson. Have you heard the news?" I then asked, "Is it Monsignor Fred Ryan?" She said, "Yes." Then I said, "Is it Bobby Martin?" She said, "Yes, how did you know?" I told her that I thought the day would come when Bobby Martin would go public in the Boston media about sexual abuse by Monsignor Fred Ryan. I then asked Millie if Sean Brady had gone public also, but she said no. Monsignor Fred Ryan (most often called Father Fred) was mid-height with flat, black, thinning hair. He was a bit nerdy and endeared himself to teenagers through his aggressive personality and use of the clerical collar to get his way. He was famous for hitting kids in a supposedly playful manner, and the kids couldn't tell the difference between playing and inappropriate touching.

Bobby Martin was a student of mine at Catholic Memorial High School in Boston. I was the faculty advisor to the football program, and Bobby was an exceptional football player. He also was a very handsome young man. He had a checkered history as a young boy, having gotten into scraps with the authorities and been forced to live on the streets because there was some trouble at home. Bobby often slept under a bridge near the school.

I had been transferred as a religious Brother from Rice High School in Harlem, New York, to New England in 1981, and so I got to know Bobby Martin because of his participation in the football program. However, I also noticed that a priest was often hanging around the varsity team, and he usually had a camera hanging around his neck. Since the head coach of the team, Hank Cutting, a gentleman par excellence, Vietnam veteran, and history teacher, had asked me to monitor the locker room after football practices because there were probably one hundred students in the locker room and supervision was needed, I saw the priest come into the locker room one time, and even into the shower room. I asked one of the students why Father Fred would be in the shower room, and he told me that he was massaging one of the player's backs. I was flabbergasted.

How I became the faculty advisor to the football program is a story in itself. I had moved into the Christian Brothers' residence in August, 1981. Soon after, I heard the telephone ringing. There were two telephone booths in the brothers' house, one on each floor. I answered the phone, "Christian Brothers, Catholic Memorial High School." The person on the other end was one of the football staff members who was calling from Maine, where the football camp was being conducted. He asked me if I could get in touch with the family of Ben Armstrong, a quarterback, who sustained an injury. I told him I would do whatever was needed even though I was brand new to the school. I found a list of students' names, addresses, and phone numbers in the phone booth, and Armstrong was on the first or second page. I was relieved to find it there. I phoned his parents immediately in a local town and informed them that they needed to call the football staff immediately.

Shortly thereafter, the camp ended, and Father Fred showed up in the brothers' community room where the headmaster and a few other Christian Brothers were relaxing and talking. When Father Fred entered the room, the headmaster stood, so I stood, and I was introduced to him (even though I already knew him from the Christian Brothers novitiate in the Hudson Valley of New York, where the football program held camp one summer when I was a novice). Father Fred then asked the headmaster, "Will Brother Robert be the faculty moderator of the football program?" The headmaster responded, "Sure, Father, if he wants to be." I told them I had been an athletic director and coach in other schools, and I said, "Sure, I'll be the football moderator. It will help me get to know the students right away."

When Hank Cutting, the head coach, asked me to supervise the locker room after practices and games, I began to sit just inside the locker room so I could keep my eye on the one hundred or so student/athletes who crowded that room every day during football season. One day, as I sat on the bench opposite the locker of co-captain Glenn Pappas, he turned to me and, in a tone that sounded disrespectful, uttered, "Hey, you're not like the others, are you?" I was astonished and asked him what he meant, but he didn't answer me. There were too many athletes around at the time, and he was finishing getting dressed, so I decided to let it go for a while until I could do more research.

One strange thing I did notice while supervising the locker room was the reaction of the football players to one of the Christian Brothers, Brother George Adrian Paramo, the moderator of the soccer program. Whenever he walked through the locker room, a loud, audible, foghorn-like sound could be heard throughout the room. I came to learn through speaking with football players and other members of the Catholic Memorial community that Brother George Adrian Paramo was "checking them out" sexually. Sure enough, his nickname was "Brother Pecker Checker." I began to understand what Glenn Pappas was referring to, and I made sure not to be too conspicuous in the locker room after that. The football players knew that there were sexual predators in their midst but couldn't tell anyone directly. I began to notice a real problem in the athletic program.

Several years after I left Catholic Memorial High School, I was contacted by another graduate, Jerry Sloane, who confided in me that Brother George Adrian Paramo had sexually abused him, too, in a local gymnasium. He was also abused in the school locker room by Brother Raphael Monahan. It took many years for Jerry to come to grips with what happened to him, and our non-profit charity did what it could to finance his rent, food, and other needs. I testified at Jerry's successful disability hearing. Unfortunately, Jerry Sloane died recently of the effects of having been sexually abused by at least three members of the faculty of Catholic Memorial High School. The third faculty member, Max Miller, a layman, invited Joe to his home, which was located near the school, and sexually abused him there.

Unfortunately, Brother George Adrian Paramo, Monsignor Fred Ryan, Max Miller, and Brother Raphael Monahan were not the only abusers at Catholic Memorial High School. A graduate of the school who became a priest, Father Carlos Cruz, confided in me that he had been sexually abused in Raul Castillo's apartment in a local town. Another student who was a junior at the time, Alan Young, also was abused by Castillo, who actually announced that the student was his "date" at a school dance. Castillo was allowed to resign and died several years ago.

According to some students, faculty, parents, and other staff members who confided in me about certain faculty members' behaviors, there were three who were pedophiles who occupied the locker room in the afternoons and evenings: Monsignor Fred Ryan, Brother George Adrian Paramo, and Brother Raphael Monahan. One day after football practice, I was supervising the locker room when I watched Monsignor Ryan enter the locker room and then the shower room. I was shocked and decided to take a look at what Father Fred was doing there. I asked one of the players who had just left the shower, "What is Father Fred doing in the shower room?" He responded, "Oh, he's massaging Ralph Smith's lower back injury." I responded, "What?" Ralph Smith was a burly, handsome kid, and Father Fred was touching him in the shower room. It took all of my strength to not enter that room and drag Father Fred out.

It also became the place where Brother Raphael Monahan brought freshmen who acted out in class to discipline them by ordering them to drop their pants so he could spank them. I became more and more attentive to the sexual antics of these folks and kept my eyes closely glued to the adults who surrounded themselves with good-looking boys. I only wish I had pursued Glenn Pappas' concern more seriously. What held me back? It was my first few weeks in the school, and I didn't think I knew enough about what was going on. I should have allowed my gut to determine my actions.

My distress and concern with Father Fred became too much, so I approached the headmaster and told him what I saw and feared. I told him that Father Fred was creepy and tended to spend his time around the best-looking football players. I protested that he spoke about sex too often at what were unaffectionately known by all as the "kick-ass" Masses, which he held before every game. His admonitions to the players during his homilies had to do with their behavior with their girlfriends on dates or elsewhere. What he was doing, in my mind, was drawing the good-looking students to himself. Father Fred was obsessed with sex.

Father (that's what most students called him rather than Monsignor) Fred Ryan took the four football captains at least twice each year to his favorite restaurant, a popular spot for Italian food in the north end of Boston. Why that restaurant? I came to understand—because I was invited there by Father Fred, too—that his favorite restaurant served wine in carafes with the Coca-Cola logo on the outside. For Father Fred, this was perfect; it allowed the minors to drink plenty of wine because it seemed to others who were dining there that they were merely drinking Coca-Cola. Father Fred plied the captains with wine and then took them back to his private suite of rooms in the headquarters of the archdiocese.

The headquarters building in which Father Fred lived was a multi-storied brick structure with an underground garage. Father Fred drove the captains in his privately-owned car into the private driveway and garage located at headquarters. No one would know what was happening because Father Fred used his remote garage device to enter the garage. What was secret was who was in the car or who was getting out of the car, except if other clergymen who lived there had been in the garage or on the elevator. The elevator was accessible directly from the underground garage, and it took Father Fred and the captains directly up to Father Fred's suite of rooms. The captains were trapped like rats.

Even though the students at Catholic Memorial High School and the staff called Father Fred "Father," his title technically was "Monsignor." He was named Vice Chancellor of the archdiocese by Cardinal Bernard Law after he left the school as chaplain in the late 1970s. He was replaced by another archdiocesan priest, Father Ronald Peters, but his position was often ignored by Father Fred, who returned regularly to size up his next prey. Father Fred's office was at the chancery of the archdiocese, but he often showed up at the school with his camera to take pictures of the football players and other athletes. He also drove the team bus to away games until I made sure to get a bus license to keep Father Fred away from the kids.

On one particular evening, I entered the school from the brothers' residence to do some copying of test materials for the next day. Standing in the lobby was one of the co-captains that year, Patrick McMahon. I asked Patrick, "Hey, Pat, what brings you to school tonight?" Pat was a guard and linebacker on the football team who became an outstanding athlete in his senior year. He was a popular captain and kept the locker room laughing with his dry humor. He was a fine kid. Pat said to me, "I'm waiting for Father Fred. He's taking the captains to Boston to his favorite restaurant tonight for the annual captains' dinner." I became suspicious but didn't let Pat know what I was thinking.

Later that evening, I was in the school for some other reason, and I saw Patrick standing outside the school. I exited the school lobby to the outdoor plaza and said to him, "How was your dinner tonight?" Pat was coy about telling me too much, but he did say, "After dinner, we went to Father Fred's apartment, and he asked us to put on doctors' coats." I said, "What? What was that about?" "He took pictures of us." Patrick was not the same kid I knew from school every day as he stood outside speaking with me. I asked him, "Can you talk about what happened?" He said, "No." I was furious at what he told me, and I imagined what happened to those four students that night.

I found out through at least two of Father Fred's victims that he had a proclivity of ordering the captains to remove various parts of their clothing and put on "costumes" that he had in his closet in his suite of rooms. One of the costumes was a doctor's coat. Why he had doctors coats in his suite of rooms could have only been for one purpose—to have the football players strip down, put on the coats, and become objects of sexual gratification for him. He took numerous photos of these young men.

Bobby Martin was one of the many captains who was subjected to Father Fred's grooming and ultimately, his sexual abuse. He noticed that one entire wall of Father Fred's sitting room was covered with photos of Catholic Memorial High School students in various states of dress and undress. Most of the students were not wearing shirts. While Father Fred held Bobby Martin and the other captains captive after plying them with alcohol, he sexually abused them. He had them disrobe completely, for example, and put on white doctors' coats and perform various actions. He told some of the students that it was his duty to measure their muscles during their four years at Catholic Memorial High School, including their genitals. He actually used a tape measure or ruler to measure their muscles. One young man was asked to disrobe and pose as "The Thinker" statue. He was naked at the time.

After I received the phone call from Millie Hudson, I went into overdrive because I sensed during my time in New England (1981–1985) that Father Fred Ryan was a serial predator. Millie Hudson had two sons in the school when I was there. Her husband owned a lucrative private company in Massachusetts, and Millie worked with me in raising money for the school.

As mentioned earlier, Father Fred had been the chaplain of the school in the 1970s, and my fears that he may have had hundreds of victims while at the school increased. He left Catholic Memorial High School around 1979 when Cardinal Bernard Law promoted him to Vice Chancellor, supposedly in charge of insurance. This was confirmed to me by one of Ryan's victims who had frequent contact with Ryan through the insurance office at the Archdiocese. In hindsight, it is my belief he was named Vice Chancellor because Cardinal Law was getting reports of Father Fred abusing teenage boys at Catholic Memorial High School, at the parish where Father Fred lived in Boston, and high school students from a number of high schools who were his parishioners but attended schools, both public and Catholic, throughout Boston and its suburbs. Father Fred Ryan was a monster predator of high school boys.

I felt terrible about Bobby Martin after I hung up from Millie Hudson, partly because Bobby was the last student in 1985 to say goodbye to me when I was transferred back to New York State to finish my doctoral degree at Fordham University. For quite some time, I felt Bobby wanted to tell me about the abuse but couldn't, and I sensed his coming to the school on a day off in late June to say goodbye to me was another way of him hinting that he wanted to stay connected so he might eventually report Father Fred's abuse.

From my office in New Jersey, the day I received the phone call from Millie Hudson, I began to try to find Bobby. I phoned one of the Christian Brothers in New England whom I still knew, Brother Matt Cawley. Brother Matt Cawley was a Catholic Memorial High School graduate and taught math at his alma mater. He was also the assistant athletic director. I phoned the school and asked for Brother Matt Cawley. They put me through to his athletic office. Brother Cawley knew Bobby from having lifted weights with him at a local gym, so I thought he might have some information for me. Brother Cawley was a jock and a weightlifter. He played the Massachusetts lottery every day, went to the gym often, and was a rabid sports fan, especially of the Red Sox and Boston Celtics. He was beloved by his students because he was a funny, but no-nonsense, teacher of math. He made math fun and understandable.

Brother Matt Cawley was also my high school debate and oratory coach in the 1960s, and we were good friends for many years. At one point during my time at Catholic Memorial High School, I asked to see him in his room to confront him about his excessive drinking. He took it well, but I think it drove a bit of a stake between us. In the meantime, his eyesight was deteriorating, and his health was, too. He died not too long after I spoke to him and received Bobby Martin's phone number, which he gave me.

Brother Cawley told me that Bobby Martin was living in the Boston area with his family. I phoned Bobby immediately. He answered the phone, and I expressed my sincerest sympathies and told him how proud I was of him for being so courageous. I then apologized to him. He asked me why I was apologizing to him. I told him I had told the headmaster in 1981 about Father Fred and my suspicions, but I did not scream loudly enough. I apologized for not making a scene about what I sensed was happening to students at Catholic Memorial High School, especially the good-looking football players.

Bobby Martin told me I did not have to apologize and that he was thrilled I phoned him. I then asked him a very important question that had played on my mind for twenty years. I asked, "Bobby, do you know anything about Sean Brady and his whereabouts?" I had a feeling that Sean was one of Father Fred's victims, and Bobby quickly responded, "Bob, you're not going to believe this, but I am sitting outside Sean's house right now. He called me as soon as he saw me on television and in the newspapers, and he said to me, 'Bobby, me too.'"

When I spoke to Bobby Martin by telephone as he sat outside Sean Brady's house, I asked him to give Sean my regards, concern, support, and phone number. I told Bobby I would go to New England once a week on my day off to help him and Sean recover from their sexual abuse. Part of my offer came from the guilt I was feeling for not speaking up more loudly when I reported Father Fred to the headmaster, Brother Declan Smith, in 1981, and asked him to ban Father Fred from the campus. The headmaster only knew Father Fred to be an exemplary priest.

The headmaster was not the only one who thought Father Fred was a great priest. Most graduates, parents, faculty, and students of the school who knew Father Fred thought he was one of the finest priests in the archdiocese. He presided at many Catholic Memorial High School weddings, funerals, baptisms, and school Masses, which were attended by hundreds of Catholic Memorial High School-connected persons.

I nearly began to cry when I heard that Sean was one of the victims, too, because he was a freshman in my first homeroom at Catholic Memorial High School in 1981. Sean sat in the first row, third seat, and I noticed that he was physically bigger than the other freshmen. I also noticed that Sean was as good-looking a kid as I had ever seen. He had Tom Cruise good looks, even better. Bobby and Sean were, perhaps, the two best-looking students in the school. Because of what I called "my abuse antenna," I could tell that Bobby and Sean were targets of the pedophile priests and brothers. I was right. I could kick myself for not protecting them better.

Sean Brady was the quarterback on the freshman football team during the 1981–82 season, but I was unaware that he had been recruited by the hockey coach to play hockey, his supposed best sport. I was furious when I heard the story of Sean Brady being recruited to play hockey because he never should have left his town's school system. He was in classes in his school that met his needs, and Catholic Memorial High School did not have those programs. Sean admitted to me courageously that he had trouble learning to read and that Catholic Memorial High School was challenging for him. Sean Brady and his tragic history is the quintessential reason why kids should not be recruited at the elementary and middle school levels to play sports. It can ruin their lives, like it ruined Sean's. Had he not attended Catholic Memorial High School, he never would have met Father Fred Ryan.

Word around the school was that Sean Brady was a guaranteed NHL player if he stayed healthy. Father Fred made sure he did not stay healthy. Sean was brought up to the varsity football team in 1982 to kick field goals at the annual Thanksgiving Day game against Boston College High School, which often drew ten thousand or more people to a university stadium. It was exciting for me as well since I had the honor of doing the public address coverage of the game. The fact that he was brought up to the varsity level to kick field goals was another indication of Sean's athletic prowess. It was around that time that Sean's personality changed completely.

As soon as Sean's freshman season ended and he was practicing with the varsity for the Thanksgiving Day game, Father Fred noticed him. Father Fred didn't attend the freshman games, or else Sean may have been targeted long before the week of Thanksgiving. After varsity practice one afternoon, Father Fred was hanging around with his camera and noticed Sean waiting outside the front door of the school for a ride from his mother. Father Fred approached Sean and asked him if he was waiting for a ride. Sean said, "Yes, Father." Father Fred then said, "Why not call your mother and tell her that I will drive you home?"

Sean called his mother and told her that the school's priest volunteered to drive him home but that he was going to take him for something to eat first. Of course, his mother was thrilled that the priest was paying attention to her son and being so nice, so she gave Father Fred permission. Father Fred took Sean to his favorite Italian restaurant and followed the same pattern as with the captains of the football team, taking Sean to his apartment after dinner. Sean was not used to having priests around, since he was a public-school kid, so when Father Fred drove him to his living quarters, he wondered what it was about. Sean was led to believe that Father Fred was helping him when Father Fred instructed him to strip down, have his muscles measured with a measuring tape, and then pose as "The Thinker" so he could be photographed. Sean was traumatized by the time the evening was over, and he sobered up on the drive home, but he was unable to tell his parents what happened to him that night and for decades to come.

CHAPTER TWO

SEAN AND JOEY

After the first incident, Father Fred had Sean trapped. He phoned him one time to say that he wanted to take him to Cape Cod for the day. Sean didn't know what to say or do. He wanted nothing to do with Father Fred, but he didn't know how to say no to a priest. Sean came up with a plan. He asked his best friend, Joey Pisano, a public school student, to go with him and Father Fred. Joey Pisano (everyone except his mother and father knew him as Joey) was as handsome a kid as Sean Brady and Bobby Martin. He was a local high school student, like Sean, but Joey was not as athletically gifted as Sean. Joey played hockey and hung out with Sean and many other local kids on the railroad tracks in town. Sean and Joey were inseparable friends until they both met Father Fred.

Sean was convinced that Father Fred would never try to sexually abuse them together. He thought both of them would be safe during the trip. He was wrong. Before the threesome headed to Cape Cod, Father Fred took Sean and Joey to a tattoo parlor in another state. Joey got an Irish tattoo, but Sean was convinced by Father Fred to get a tattoo of a devil on his upper thigh. Both of them were thrilled to get tattoos, but Sean was angry that his tattoo was of a devil. *Why would Father Fred do that?* he asked himself. After leaving the tattoo parlor, the two boys thought they were on their way to Cape Cod, but Father Fred had other plans.

Father Fred stopped at a liquor store and bought enough booze to last the day and night. Sean and Joey thought the next stop was a beach on Cape Cod where they might spend the day on the beach drinking, sunbathing, and swimming. Father Fred's deceit kicked in, however. He took the boys to a motel in a neighboring state, and began a day and night of terror. All three quickly began drinking heavily, and before long, the boys felt no pain, which gave this priest his signal. He took each one into the motel bathroom and sexually abused them.

Father Fred finally had his fill of alcohol and fell asleep. Joey and Sean saw their chance to retaliate and dumped potato chips all over his body and then urinated on his stomach. Father Fred never woke up. Sean and Joey then concocted a plan to kill Father Fred and dump his body in a ditch near the motel. What stopped them? Father Fred's car and its distance from the motel entrance. Father Fred drove an older car with a personalized license plate, which was well-known to many. Joey and Sean could not figure out how to kill him, drag the body to the front entrance, and haul it to his distant car, where they could drive his body to a ditch. So, they went to sleep, got up the next morning, and Father Fred drove them home to their town. As Sean reported, there was hardly a word spoken on the ride home.

Sean did suit up for the Thanksgiving Day game and got through the holiday weekend. However, his life had been altered forever. He returned to school a different person. I noticed in homeroom that he was distant and preoccupied. Since I didn't teach him, I didn't notice if he was misbehaving in class, but I heard from the dean of students and others that Sean was missing school, skipping classes, and acting out. His grades cratered, and he was in danger of failing out. This wonderful, respectful, handsome, athletic ninth grader had changed completely. He ended up leaving the school before the end of freshman year but after the varsity hockey season at Catholic Memorial High School. He played varsity hockey as a freshman, and some of the older kids saw the writing on the wall because Sean was taking their places on various lines. However, he got into trouble with his coach and parents when he refused to accompany the hockey team to Maine to play a game against a high school team there. He refused to go because he heard through locker-room talk that Father Fred was going to be the bus driver.

There was no way he was going to Maine on a bus driven by his sexual abuser.

Sean eventually left Catholic Memorial High School and joined the hockey program at his local town's high school, but his potential as a star in the NHL eroded quickly because of the effects of the sexual abuse. He started to drink heavily and snort cocaine. He began to not care about life, family, school, or sports.

It was my discussion with Bobby Martin, sitting outside Sean's house that night, and my eventual lengthy conversation with Sean that gave birth to my non-profit organization. I asked both Bobby and Sean if they would like me to go to New England on my day off to help them recover from the nightmares they experienced. They jumped at the idea, and my weekly trips to counsel them, beginning in March, 2002, convinced me that clergy sexual abuse victim/survivors needed ongoing advocacy and help.

Since I had a full-time, Monday-through-Friday job as Director of Schools of Our Lady of Good Counsel Parish where I spent ten to twelve hours per day because of its challenges, I tried to get to New England on weekends, even though I worked in two to three parishes on weekends as well. I often left New Jersey at noon on a Sunday, met Bobby and Sean for a few hours, and then returned to New Jersey that same night. Non-school days permitted me to spend more time with Bobby and Sean, and those days were especially beneficial. What I was being taught was that clergy sexual abuse victim/survivors needed a host of services, including advocacy, social and mental health services, and basic human needs, like food and clothing.

In approximately April, 2002, after working with Bobby and Sean for a few weeks and being transformed by their courage and determination to seek justice, I began to feel more courageous myself. Then I learned about another act of courage. Sean Brady had gone public in a very dramatic way. Shortly after Bobby Martin appeared in the media with his story and then was contacted by Sean, they both, with their supporters, stood outside a State House, where Sean talked generally about the sexual abuse he endured in that state. Joey Pisano was supposed to attend and did accompany the group, but he couldn't take the pressure and did not appear before the public. He hid in a car parked near the State House. I would not begin to help Joey Pisano for several months after Sean's request that I get involved with helping his best friend, Joey.

Sean Brady brought a beautiful son, Zachary, into the world in the early 2000s. Zachary, a college student, is a proficient bowler who has bowled a 300 game several times while still in his teens. Sean and Zachary see each other often. Ironically, it might turn out that the son of the prospective NHL player might become the professional in the family as a member of the Professional Bowlers Association. Sean attends many bowling matches throughout Florida and the country, cheering on his son.

In 2018, I received a telephone call from Fort Lauderdale, Florida, regarding Sean's health. His condition was critical. He did not realize that a urological problem would have such deleterious effects on his kidneys, and they were failing fast. A superb nephrologist saved his life during the first emergency, and Sean began to recover. However, the recovery would be temporary. His kidneys did fail, and Sean required a transplant. He phoned me late one night to report that a kidney was available at a Florida hospital, but the kidney was a Hepatitis C kidney. I was told by Sean that Hepatitis C kidneys are extracted from those whose health has declined for a number of reasons, often overdoses or regular drug use. The doctors recommended that Sean accept the kidney, since they could cure the Hep-C in six to eight weeks. I advised Sean to take the kidney, and he courageously headed to the hospital for the transplant. I got in my car and headed to Miami. I saw Sean the day after the transplant surgery, and he looked like a new man. His color returned to his face and he was himself again.

The sexual abuse of Sean Brady ended after two terrifying episodes, one in Father Fred's suite of rooms, and one in a run-down motel, but the sexual abuse of Joey Pisano continued for many, many years. Sean Brady pleaded with me in the early 2000s to help Joey, who he thought was near death because of his drug and alcohol addictions. It turned out that Father Fred had turned Joey on to illegal drugs in the motel and elsewhere. Sean felt bad that he had invited Joey on the supposed trip to Cape Cod. He never thought Father Fred would sexually abuse two teenage boys together on the same trip, but neither boy knew the power of manipulation by pedophile priests.

I found the telephone number of the Pisano family in a Boston suburb, and I phoned the Pisanos one day, in approximately 2002, and introduced myself. Joey's mother, Angie, answered the phone, and I introduced myself. "Mrs. Pisano," I said, "my name is Father Bob Hoatson, and I have been working with Sean Brady and Bobby Martin regarding their sexual abuse by Father Fred Ryan. I was informed that your son, Joey, may have experienced similar abuse to that of Sean and Bobby Martin. I have been helping them for the past few months, and I would like to offer my help to Joey as well."

What I heard next led me to tears once again, as both Mr. and Mrs. Pisano got on the phone at various times during the call, telling me that their son was close to death and that they did not expect him to make it much longer. Mrs. Pisano described the time her husband and she had to cut down their son from their garage as he attempted to hang himself and that he had been in and out of prison and rehab for years. They were at their wits' end and could not even allow their son to live in their house because they feared his violent temper.

They told me they would give my message to Joey, and I told them I would meet him at the gas station a few blocks from their home on Sunday, which happened to be either Super Bowl Sunday or the semifinals. I left New Jersey after my final Mass and arrived in the Boston suburbs a little after noon. I sat for several minutes in the gas station's parking lot and was about to leave when I noticed a good-looking man approaching my car. It was Joey Pisano. He got into the car, and we introduced ourselves. I asked him where he wanted to go to talk. He said, "Let's go to Bruno's for pizza." I said, "Fine with me." He clearly was as nervous as I was. I didn't know what to expect. He seemed okay when we drove to Bruno's, which was about a fifteen-minute drive.

While we were at Bruno's, Joey excused himself at least four times to use the men's room. Each time he returned, his mood was more and more mellow, and he was high as a kite by the time we finished our meals. He may have eaten a slice of pizza, if that. He was doing heroin in the men's room. I was patient and realized the higher he got, the more he was able to talk. The story he told me was very basic (victims never tell the whole story when they first meet an advocate or a therapist). What he did tell me, though, was horrific enough, including the fact that Father Fred turned him on to illegal drugs and that he was an addict since that day at the motel. He then went on his way, higher than ever.

The story of Joey Pisano and his relationship with our non-profit organization spanned nearly fifteen years, and it continues to this day, on and off. For the first several years, we stayed in close touch, and I would usually pick him up and take him to a restaurant so we could talk. He opened up slowly but completely during those years. He began to trust me to the point that he couldn't believe I was a priest who didn't want to have sex with him.

Joey told me that he had been in prison dozens of times over the years and in rehab at least fifty times. One doctor allegedly told one of his friends that he never saw a human being take as much heroin as Joey did and live. That fact, and associated behaviors connected to addictions, led to Joey's frequent incarcerations in several correctional houses. Those facilities became his home for many months and years. On one occasion, Joey was released from prison, where I had visited him frequently and deposited money in his canteen, and he agreed to go to a halfway house in order to break his drug habit. I dropped him off the day before Thanksgiving, and he was out of there by the day after Thanksgiving. I went to a town on the south shore of Boston to pick him up and, in my best "tough love" stance, said, "What the hell happened?" He said, "I didn't like the attitude of one of the clients, so I clocked him and knocked him out." I responded, "What now, Joey? You have no place to live and no money."

During our aimless car ride around Massachusetts, I tried to convince Joey to report the sexual abuse of Father Fred to the archdiocese so they could start offering him recovery services. He said, "Pull into the Dunkin' Donuts ahead." I complied, and we began to talk seriously. When I told Joey that he was going to eventually have to confront the abuse and get help, he pulled a butcher knife out of his duffel bag and put it to my neck. I said, "Joey, you're not going to hurt me. You have to make a decision. Let me drive you to talk to the archdiocese." He declined but put the knife away.

We sat silently in the Dunkin' Donuts parking lot for a few minutes when Joey said, "Let's go visit my relative at his hair salon down the street." I drove the car about a mile, and Joey said, "There it is." I turned into the parking lot, and we went into the salon. Joey's relative had a thriving women's hair salon, and he and Joey had a social relationship with each other, taking trips to Connecticut casinos where they, at times, would gamble the night away.

As we entered the salon, Joey's Uncle Billy greeted us as he cleaned up from the day's work. Joey and I each sat in one of the salon chairs, and Billy asked us why we were there. Joey said he had been kicked out of rehab and that we were not sure where he was going to go. We then discussed the possibility of my driving Joey to the archdiocese so he could report the sexual abuse he experienced from Father Fred, and Joey lost it again. He took scissors from the counter in front of the salon chair he was sitting in and threatened to take out both Billy and me. Once again, I told Joey he wasn't going to hurt anybody and that he needed to make a decision.

Finally, he blurted out, "Okay, I will go to the archdiocese. Let's go." Immediately, I got up and started out the door so he couldn't change his mind. He followed me out the door to my car, and off we went to a Boston suburb, where the archdiocese had an office to help victims of clergy sexual abuse. We met with the director of the office, Anne Sloane, and another social worker, Andrea Kim, and Joey told them the story of Father Fred Ryan abusing him for almost fifteen years. Toward the end, I explained to Anne and Andrea that Joey needed a place to stay since he was expelled from the rehab center and asked them to allow me to place him in a hotel for a week or so at my cost initially, with a promise that the archdiocese would reimburse me. It took me weeks and weeks of emails and finally a letter to Cardinal Sean O'Malley to receive my reimbursement, but Joey Pisano at least had a place to stay. It was up to him to work with social service agencies to find a place to live on a more permanent basis.

Fortunately, the abscess that had ailed Joey Pisano for so many years had been pierced. One of the benefits of going to the archdiocese was the ability to arrange for Joey to see a therapist on a regular basis. Joey chose a therapist, and he began the process of recovery. Believe it or not, Joey stopped taking heroin "cold turkey," which, medically, is nearly impossible. However, he did not quit other substances, which still remains a challenge. I was hopeful that he might continue recovering if he remained consistent with his therapy sessions. His recovery has been a roller coaster of ups, downs, and sideways, even to the present. I receive calls from Joey approximately every six months, and he called me in November, 2020, after his father, Henry, died.

CHAPTER THREE

BOBBY, SEAN, AND VINCE

At the same time that I was helping Joey Pisano, my trips to New England to work with Sean Brady and Bobby Martin on their recoveries continued. Our meetings were sometimes in groups and other times one on one. I am not a psychotherapist; rather, I am a pastoral counselor from my training to become a priest. Both Sean and Bobby were dealing with various addictions, mainly alcohol and opiates. Sean worked for several years in construction, including a famous Boston redevelopment project. Sean descended hundreds of feet every day into construction projects to help the city redevelop. Fortunately, his father was in the same business and helped his son learn the construction trade. Sean earned a good salary and had health benefits, which were especially important for the baby he had on the way.

Bobby Martin had a number of employments, including more than one entrepreneurial enterprise. He had a large family to support. His son, Devin, his only boy, began skating at a young age. Bobby, a very good hockey player, taught him everything he knew, so Devin was an exceptional hockey player, even in his elementary school days. He became a star both in Canada and the U.S.A. as a member of the NHL. Like Sean Brady, whose son might be the professional in his sport, bowling, Bobby, who was recruited to play in the NHL, is enjoying watching his son succeed in his profession. Bobby was trained and mentored by professionals, including some well-known and famous players. Bobby Martin followed in the footsteps of his good friend and fellow Catholic Memorial High School High graduate, Vince LeRoy, who played for a couple of professional teams and was known as a powerful hockey player. Vince and Bobby were good friends for a long time, and Father Fred Ryan showed an interest in both men's athletic careers.

Robert M. Hoatson, Ph.D.

Vince LeRoy had been retired from the National Hockey League for a few years when Bobby went public in 2002 with his story of sexual abuse by Father Fred Ryan. Vince LeRoy, who lived near Catholic Memorial High School, was a friend of Father Fred Ryan. Vince LeRoy developed his hockey skills on the MDC rinks of the city of Boston and at Catholic Memorial High School. Bobby Martin lived on the same street as Vince, and had a mentor in the same neighborhood and within sight of Catholic Memorial High School. However, hockey and Father Fred Ryan brought them closer and closer as the years went on.

Because I was helping Sean and Bobby recover from their sexual abuse, I knew that Vince LeRoy might have been a big help to me. I especially was interested in his knowledge of Father Fred, which might have helped me as I worked with Sean and Bobby on their recoveries. I called him one day and asked, "Vince, did Father Fred give you any hints that he was a pedophile priest?" He answered, "Not at all," and I was relieved. I asked if he thought Bobby was a victim of Father Fred, and he said he didn't think so. Vince and I remained in contact until he moved out of the country, where he has become an inspirational speaker and radio celebrity, helping young people develop healthy lifestyles.

Vince LeRoy became integral in the cases of Sean Brady and Bobby Martin because of their connection to hockey, Catholic Memorial High School, and Father Fred Ryan. Vince spoke to Sean Brady from time to time, offering his support and advice, and Vince and Bobby continued their close friendship. It was tested one day shortly after Bobby had his fill of Father Fred Ryan in an incident that could have ended in tragedy.

Bobby Martin was living in a beautiful home in a leafy suburb several miles south of Boston. He had been a successful sales agent and was doing well financially. He even donated an expensive copier to Catholic Memorial High School, despite the fact that the school did nothing to help him recover from Father Fred's sexual abuse.

Once Bobby Martin had gone public many years ago, his trauma was triggered from time to time with memories of the abuse, and one day, he had enough. He got into his sports car and headed to Chadwick, a working-class town north of Boston. Father Fred Ryan was living there in his family's home, after Cardinal Sean O'Malley removed him from ministry. Next to Bobby in the passenger seat was a meat cleaver. He was heading to Chadwick to seriously harm Monsignor Fred, his abuser.

Fortunately, a member of Bobby's family who had a clue as to what he was up to, reportedly phoned the police department, and reported what Bobby was about to do. Vince LeRoy also learned about what Bobby was about to do, and he headed to Chadwick as well. A few days before Bobby plotted to harm Father Fred, Vince LeRoy phoned Father Fred and asked him to admit what he had done sexually to Bobby, Sean, and others. Father Fred reportedly signed a sheet of paper, admitting that he had sexually abused many former students and indicating their names on the sheet of paper. He was ready to turn it over to Vince LeRoy. Vince went to Father Fred's house to get the sheet of paper, but just before he handed it over, he pulled it back and never gave it to Vince. Vince was furious and let Father Fred know what he thought of him. Vince could see the partial list in Father Fred's hand, and it definitely contained a list of names.

As Bobby made his way to Chadwick, the media were listening to the police scanners that were busily reporting the planned incident in Chadwick. Reporters, such as WQD television's Art Wilson, who was well-known to Vince LeRoy, took up positions near Father Fred's house. Bobby traveled over the famous Stonewall Bridge, which connects the city with its northern suburbs, and was a few minutes from Chadwick. As he crossed into Chadwick, the police were on his tail as he approached the Ryan house. Before Bobby could even get out of his car, the police surrounded it and took him out of the car. An ambulance had been called to the scene as well, and Bobby was placed on a gurney and put in the ambulance. The next morning, newspapers ran a front-page photograph of Bobby being placed in the ambulance and being whisked away to McLean Hospital for psychiatric evaluation.

Bobby's convalescence at McLean Hospital may have saved his life because he met a world-renowned doctor there who treated trauma and other sexual abuse-related symptoms. Bobby recommended the doctor to Sean Brady as well. I recommended the McLean Hospital professionals to Joey Pisano, too. It turned out that Bobby's crisis in Chadwick led to all three men getting help for their sexual abuse. All three men were inordinately courageous and committed to recovery. They wanted the demons to stop.

I was concerned that the money our non-profit was giving Joey Pisano for necessities was being used for drugs and alcohol, so I decided to consult with one of the doctors at McLean Hospital for advice. Without hesitation, the psychiatrist said to me, "Father Bob, the money you are giving to Joey might be the best money you are spending from your charity." I was astonished. I asked him to explain. He responded, "The drugs Joey is buying with your money are keeping him alive right now. He is using drugs to slow down his head and not make his condition worse. Keep helping him with money, and he will eventually not need those drugs. Right now, his brain needs them. Be patient." Sure enough, the doctor was correct, and Joey eventually began using legal medications to assist him with his trauma.

Had Catholic Memorial High School alumna parent Millie Hudson not phoned my office in New Jersey in 2002 and told me about Bobby Martin going public with his sexual abuse, I may have never connected again with Bobby, Sean Brady, or Joey Pisano. I also may have never met Vince LeRoy. Millie Hudson is a close friend whose two sons, Jerry and Jamie, attended Catholic Memorial High School and whose husband, Francis, was as active and helpful to the school as she. Millie and Francis joined two other couples, whose dedication to the school was nothing short of heroic. In 1982, I was appointed Assistant Headmaster for Development, which meant I was in charge of adding to the endowment of the school.

The three couples began to help raise significant funds for the school. We sponsored an annual lottery whereby we sold three hundred tickets at $150 each and gave away a top prize of $10,000. By the time I left the school in 1985, the fundraising team had raised over $100,000 through the Lottery and the Mothers' Club Christmas Bazaar, which raised approximately $25,000 annually. I left the school in June, 1985 to pursue my doctoral degree at Fordham University, but my re-connection with Bobby and Sean and others in the early 2000s made it feel like I had never left.

Robert M. Hoatson, Ph.D.

CHAPTER FOUR

IT WAS MY TURN TO COME FORWARD

Were it not for the courage of Bobby Martin and Sean Brady, I may never have told anyone about the sexual abuse I suffered. The fact that Bobby Martin would stand before the media in Boston and then convince Sean (and Joey at first) to stand in front of a State Capitol to speak about past sexual abuse—I knew I had to speak out. But make no mistake: my courage was increasing throughout 2002, so I decided to tell someone my story of both sexual abuse by members of the Christian Brothers and another traumatic event in my life.

I chose to speak to Msgr. Kenneth Lasch, pastor of Saint Joseph's Parish in suburban New Jersey, who supported, at first, a young man and then many young men from his parish who were sexually abused by Father Ken's predecessor, Father James Hanley. I met Father Ken in his parish and finally spilled my guts in their entirety for the first time. Msgr. Kenneth Lasch's official title was Monsignor Kenneth Lasch, but his humility motivated him to tell people to call him Father Ken. He told me before we started our conversation that he had decided to profess a preferential option for victim/survivors of clergy sexual abuse, and his parish homilies reminded his parishioners of his preference each and every Sunday. Many of his homilies contained information and stories about fellow parishioners who were damaged by priests, especially his predecessor, and that it was the parish's responsibility to help restore the men to wholeness. Of course, I was impressed and knew I was speaking to the right person.

I communicated to Father Ken that when I was approximately 14 years old, my mother, sister, and I were in a fairly large department store in my hometown in New Jersey. I had to go to the men's room, so I told my mother I would meet her in a certain section of the store after I left the bathroom. While I was doing my business at a urinal, an adult male walked in and occupied the urinal next to me. He reached his hand toward my penis in order to grab it, and I was able to block his movement with my forearm. I pulled up my zipper and ran out of the bathroom. There was a security guard outside the men's room, but I couldn't tell him. I was much too afraid. I found my mother and sister, but I could not tell them either. I kept this information to myself until I told Father Ken.

I told Father Ken that several months later, during my first year of high school in 1966, and whose population was over two thousand students, I was asked to work at an alumni event. There were hundreds of men at this reunion. While I was engaged in some task at the alumni gathering, I noticed in the distance the same man who tried to grab me in the department store bathroom. My face turned pale, my stomach churned, and I made sure to stay away from him. I still couldn't tell anyone about it. I can still see that person's face and believe I could identify him if I went through school yearbooks. He had dark hair that hung over his forehead and an olive complexion. I still get horrible goosebumps when I recall his face. I wanted to run away from the alumni event, but I was afraid someone would wonder why I left so precipitously, especially the Christian Brother who asked me to work the event.

I also told Father Ken that when I entered the postulancy[1] of the Christian Brothers in 1970, a few months after high school graduation at which I received the school's highest honor, "The Foremost Essex Senior," I was groomed for sex by my trusted superior, Brother Felix O'Shaughnessy. I was on cloud nine after graduation in June, and three months later, my life would change for the worse.

Brother Felix O'Shaughnessy came from a very wealthy family and held powerful influence. As young postulants, he took us on

---

1   "First Year" of religious life

trips to the beaches of Long Island, some of which resembled the estates of Cape Cod, Hyannis Port, Massachusetts. On one trip he brought us to his family's beach home. The family also owned a home in Bermuda where Brother Felix often took his "favorite" younger brothers for rest, relaxation, and whatever. The mantra among the brothers, especially the younger ones, was that you were favored if you were one of the "O'Shaughnessy Boys." I always felt Brother Felix O'Shaughnessy used his family's wealth to promote himself within the Christian Brothers religious order.

Every month, the superior of the postulancy held a one-on-one conference with each postulant. At my first monthly conference, which was held shortly after I entered the postulancy, Brother Felix O'Shaughnessy told me, "Bob, you are a cold person and need warming up. We need to warm you up." My response, at first, was shock because I never considered myself to be a cold person. I had lots of high school friends, both male and female, and I was involved in every aspect of life at my high school. In addition, I thought that anyone who wanted to be a brother or a priest must have some warmth if they wanted to respond to a religious vocation. What did Brother Felix O'Shaughnessy mean?

I was confused and concerned about what Brother Felix O'Shaughnessy told me. It took me until I was in talk therapy years later to realize that Brother Felix's comments were a sexual "come-on." I actually believed, because he was the superior, that I might have a flaw in my character. I wanted to be a good, holy brother, so I began a process of unhealthy introspection. I was very hard on myself for being cold. I began to wonder if I had to have sex with the superior in order to prove my warmth. Brother Felix O'Shaughnessy continued the same mantra that year, but he never actually touched me sexually.

Msgr. Kenneth Lasch was visibly disgusted with what I told him about Brother O'Shaughnessy. He was not surprised and expressed to me that he had heard similar stories of seminarians and other religious superiors. He learned from me that Brother Felix O'Shaughnessy threatened to not let me move to the novitiate if he didn't see me become warmer, which made Father Ken livid. I said to him, "If you think that was bad, stay tuned."

CHAPTER FIVE

MY ONE-YEAR NOVITIATE- BOTH YEARS

Since Kenneth Lasch was a priest, he was very familiar with religious and clerical terms, so I told him next about my novice master, Brother Michael Giordano. Brother Giordano was yet another brother who used his family's wealth and his charming disposition to be favored and get ahead within the hierarchy of the Church.

My novitiate started in August, 1971, and was to last one year. Novitiate is actually a canonical term under Church law because every religious person must complete a novitiate before taking the vows of poverty, chastity, and obedience. The novitiate is a program for developing spiritually, learning the history of the religious order, studying some theology and philosophy, and spending a lot of time in meditation. Novices are supposed to begin to separate themselves from the world so they can live more fully in the spiritual life; thus, a novitiate house is ideally located in a rural area where there are few distractions.

Brother Giordano never should have been a novice master because he was a severe alcoholic. He often did not show up for the class he was supposed to teach about the religious life, including the Constitutions of the Christian Brothers, and the sub-superior, another alcoholic, often had to take his place. The novices were told that Brother Giordano had a bad back and couldn't get out of bed very often. Novitiate was a disaster. Nearly every finally vowed brother who was assigned to the novitiate had an alcohol problem, including the cook and a retired brother from the farm whose nickname was Dizzy. He was called Dizzy because he was usually tipsy. "Dizzy Izzy" could often be found on the floor or staircase sleeping it off.

Robert M. Hoatson, Ph.D.

The novitiate of the Christian Brothers, Santa Maria, was located in farm country in the Hudson Valley of New York. The hamlet had a small post office and one restaurant. That was about it. The larger town is famous for the number of religious houses that dot the old highway through New York State. There were at least six religious orders that had seminaries and religious houses on the east side of the highway along the beautiful Hudson River, including the Marist Brothers and the Redemptorist Fathers and Brothers. Msgr. Kenneth Lasch was familiar with the area I was referencing, as the Christian Brothers owned over 1,000 acres of that land at one time. The provincial cemetery is located on the property as well.

I then told Father Ken that I was sexually abused by Brother Giordano, my novice master. I was warned before going to the novitiate that Brother Giordano had a tradition of passing the keys to the jeep and the tractor to the novice who was going to be his favorite, and the novice had to be good looking. I didn't realize exactly what that meant, but it soon became clear that I was targeted by the novice master for sex. I got the keys to the jeep and the tractor. After each monthly conference with him in his office, we would stand, he would grab me tight, hug me, and rub his erect penis against my body. He wore the same aftershave lotion every day, and I still have nightmares of smelling that aftershave. I had my first major panic attack once the sexual abuse began. I knew if I said something, I would be expelled, and I wanted to be a religious brother so I kept quiet.

After my panic and anxiety increased substantially, I developed stomach problems—ulcers. I finally consulted a doctor in the area, and he asked me if my issue was stress and nervousness and not stomach problems. He was right, but I couldn't tell him that I was being sexually abused. After a few months of Brother Giordano's abuse, I decided to leave the novitiate. On leap year, 1972, February 29, I informed Brother Giordano that I would be leaving the novitiate, and my parents were called to pick me up. I left that afternoon and relaxed to a certain degree.

Father Ken was once again sad at what happened, and he asked me how I endured my postulancy and novitiate. I then told him, "Hold on, Father Ken, there's a lot more."

One of the novices who preceded me in the novitiate, who also was given the keys to the jeep and tractor, committed suicide after he was abused by Brother Giordano. Other predecessors reminded me to be careful about the predator brothers like Brother Felix O'Shaughnessy and Brother Giordano. Among the victims and "favorites" of Brothers O'Shaughnessy and Giordano, many young prospects and vowed Christian Brothers were harmed forever. Another young brother, a favorite of one of the two men mentioned above, died in his 40s. He was an athlete and scholar, and his life ended in tragedy — he drank himself to death.

Msgr. Kenneth Lasch, by now, was both sad and angry, so I had to change course with him for a few minutes and give him the background of the next abuse I endured after the sexual abuse by Brother Giordano.

I returned with my parents to New Jersey, and lived in their house. Since the spring college semester had already begun, I knew I would have to get a job and then, perhaps, start college again in the fall. Since my avocation was the game of golf, I applied for a position as a starter at a local, private country club. The golf professional was leaving for another club, and he wanted the new professional to have a starter[2] in place when he arrived. The new professional, Kevin B. Riley, was arriving in a few weeks from California. He was the 11th of 12 professionals at that country club in Los Angeles, where members included Glen Campbell. Kevin was

---
2 The person who schedules and organizes the tee times at a club

friends with club makers and manufacturers and shared all types of clubs and equipment with me.

Kevin B. Riley arrived, and he and I got along great. He named me assistant golf professional and thought I might have a great career in professional golf. Ironically, Kevin and I had the same high school golf coach. Brother Paul B. Whalen was Kevin's coach at a greater Northwest area Catholic school, and Brother Whalen was my golf coach in New Jersey. Kevin gave me numerous golf lessons and said I had one of the purest golf swings he had ever seen. His own golf swing was somewhat unorthodox, somewhat like that of successful professional Jim Furyk, and he had me hitting the ball long and straight after a fashion. Kevin wanted to sponsor me at PGA School in Florida, but I turned him down, foolishly, as I realize now. I told him I still wanted to be a Christian Brother.

That fall, I left the country club and started at Montclair State University. I wanted to accumulate credits to prepare for my return to Columba College in New York, owned and operated by the Christian Brothers. Brother Giordano had been removed as novice master, and the new novice master did not have an abusive reputation. I finished one year at Montclair State University and then re-applied to the Christian Brothers. I was accepted again and went back to the novitiate for a full year.

My new novice master, Brother Peter Morgan, was a solid guy who treated the novices with care, respect, and compassion. Brother Morgan was a tall, roundish man who played sports, even golf, and several of us played a few rounds at a local New York course. He didn't put up with any sexual acting out, and he had to expel two novices who were found making love in a closet. While my anxiety and panic returned now and then, I made it through the second novitiate with a fair amount of ease. Because I was two years older than most of the other novices, I was able to take a course at the local seminary up the road in New Testament studies. I enjoyed that break from the traditional novitiate since the professor, a priest, was an entertainer as well as a New Testament scholar. On August 9, 1974, my novitiate class took its first vows, the same day that Richard Nixon resigned as president. I recall sitting in front of the television a few hours before taking vows, watching the United States government devolve into crisis.

Robert M. Hoatson, Ph.D.

CHAPTER SIX

MY SCHOLASTICATE YEAR BROUGHT MORE ABUSE

Following the vow ceremony, I was no longer called a novice, but a scholastic, which meant I would spend the rest of my formation at Columba College finishing my degree in English. Before the fall semester began, however, my scholastic class spent nearly three weeks on vacation at the Jersey Shore with our new superior, Brother Lachlan Stafford, a hail fellow, well-met kind of guy who once said he didn't trust anyone who didn't drink. Brother Stafford was a tall man with a very approachable personality. He taught at schools in the western and eastern United States and served in a number of leadership positions. He taught at my high school when I was a student, but I did not have him for any classes. He was transferred to become the Superior in the 1970s, of the Christian Brothers' community in New England which became known as a party house. Lay people, like teachers, used the Brothers' community room in Boston, and Brother Lachlan was just fine with that. It would be naive not to mention that alcohol was an integral part of the religious life of the Christian Brothers.

As a community of about a dozen, we rented a large house in a beautiful, New Jersey Shore town, but it required that two or three of us occupied each of the five or six bedrooms in the house. My roommate, Brother Matthew Aquinas, had been a friend in the novitiate, and we continued to grow as friends. He talked often about his girlfriends and his family-owned business. My impression was that Brother Matthew Aquinas was heterosexual, and when we roomed together in the novitiate, there was never a sense that he would "try" anything with me. He had photos of his supposed girlfriend on his night table and talked frequently about her. However, he liked to smoke marijuana, but his invitations to me were always rejected. Brother Matthew Aquinas was famous for sneaking behind the novitiate and smoking marijuana. He invited me a few times, but I refused. There were others who joined him. In addition, he was losing his hair at a fairly fast rate. He eventually shaved his head completely.

One night at bedtime in the Jersey Shore house, I had gotten into bed, dressed in my usual briefs since there was no air conditioning in the house and the humidity at the Jersey Shore was high during the dog days of August. I had gotten under the top sheet and prepared for sleep when Brother Matthew pulled his chair next to my bed. He said he wanted to talk. I thought he was going to tell me that he had doubts about the vows he just took and maybe that he was going to leave the brothers.

Instead, he began to stroke my body up and down, including my genitals, and I became terrified. I couldn't say a word as he began his actions, and I froze in silence. He continued his actions until I ejaculated under my shorts. I then turned over and tried to sleep. As I told Kenneth Lasch more and more of the story, he put his hand to his head as if to say, "My God, what have we come to?"

Another thing I was fearful about was the fact the superior, Brother Lachlan Stafford, was sleeping in the next room to us; in fact, his room was sort of an annex off our larger room. There was a door separating us, but the door was never locked. I didn't know what to do, except to keep as quiet as I could. Brother Matthew Aquinas pulled the same stunt once more during vacation, and I promised myself he would not do it again. I kept my distance from him the rest of the vacation, except for social gatherings where I had to pretend and treat him as a friend.

Msgr. Kenneth Lasch was assuming, I think, that my story of Brother Matthew Aquinas might be the end of the story. I asked him to be patient with me because I was nowhere near finished.

Brother Matthew Aquinas continued his sexual abuse when we returned to Columba College at the end of August. My room at Edmund Hall, also called the Scholasticate, was part of a magnificent mansion that was able to house all twenty of us since the class ahead of ours was still there, finishing up their senior year.

My room was a large, nearly private bedroom on the second floor with a bathroom off an annex that housed another scholastic. His room was tiny but private, and I had to go through his room to get to the bathroom. One night as I tried to go to sleep, Brother Matthew Aquinas came into my room and began to stroke my body again. This lasted for several weeks, happening almost nightly, and the other scholastic had caught on that Brother Matthew Aquinas was not there for spiritual direction, even though he had never seen any specific sexual behavior on Matthew Aquinas' part. I couldn't tell anyone in authority because I feared I would be thrown out of the brothers, so the sexual abuse by Matthew Aquinas lasted approximately three years, on and off, mostly "off," thank God.

I spent one year only at Edmund Hall finishing my degree since I was older and more advanced in my studies than my class, which included Brother Matthew Aquinas. Following commencement, I was assigned to teach seventh grade at St. Columba School in East Harlem, New York City. I was thrilled to have been assigned there in a poor neighborhood. My family wasn't thrilled with my assignment, and when my parents and grandmother helped me move in to the Christian Brothers' residence in El Barrio, my nonagenarian, Scottish, non-Catholic grandmother uttered to me in her strong burr, "Oh, Bobby, you don't want to live in this neighborhood, do you?" There were young Puerto Rican kids playing in the streets, even using the front wall of the brothers' house to play handball.

Robert M. Hoatson, Ph.D.

CHAPTER SEVEN

A NEW SUPERIOR

My new superior in East Harlem was a very kind, generous man named Brother Martin Francis Connelly. Frank (he went by his religious name) was a chubby, uncoordinated man who had an effeminate type of speech. He was not into sports at all but did not get in the way of those of us who played basketball or golf or those who wanted to watch Sunday football or college basketball. My basketball team that year won the archdiocesan championship, and Frank was most supportive. I wasn't quite sure why Frank looked like he had women's breasts, but he later admitted to me (while he was abusing me) that he suffered from gynecomastia[3] and was overly self-conscious of it.

Brother Martin Francis Connelly took care of the spiritual and monetary needs of the community, and he taught eighth grade math and acted as the treasurer for the priests, who ran the parish. St. Columba Parish was so large it had two elementary schools. General Reed School was five blocks from St. Columba Church and was run by the Sisters of Mercy. Saint Columba School was located three long blocks from the parish church and was supposed to be administered by the Christian Brothers and lay teachers, but politics from the parish rectory placed a Sister of Mercy in charge. I got in trouble for questioning the entire process, and was transferred at the end of the school year as a result. Another Christian Brother, who also questioned the process, along with me, were called to headquarters and read the riot act, but we did not back down. Both of us were transferred at the end of the school year for questioning unjust authority. My seventh-grade class, which I nicknamed "Seventh Heaven," was located on the fifth-floor walk-

---

3 Swollen male breast tissue caused by a hormone imbalance

up, and the bathroom on that floor still had pull-chain toilets. The building was well over 100 years old, but I loved it.

At this point in our conversation, I asked Father Ken to hold those thoughts for a while and allow me to skip ahead a few years because my sexual abuse was semi-connected to my time in East Harlem. I asked Father Ken to jump from 1976 to approximately 1981. He assured me he was following the story.

I reminded him that my superior in East Harlem was Brother Martin Francis Connelly. During my time in El Barrio, which was only one year, I got along great with Brother Frank, and he seemed to think that one day, I would be a leader in the religious order. In May of my first year of teaching, I received a notice that I was being transferred from the inner-city to Blessed Sacrament High School in suburban New York. I was broken-hearted, and that summer was the year of sabbatical for the brothers, meaning that we were given a certain amount of vacation money and could go anywhere in the world that that money could take us.

Brother Frank decided during July to lower ceilings in the brothers' residence, and he asked me to help him. Of course, I said yes. It took one month to complete the work, and August and sabbatical vacation were upon us. Brother Frank asked me to consider driving with him to Canada, where they were celebrating the centennial of the arrival of the Christian Brothers in North America. He said there would be numerous celebrations of the brothers and that I might enjoy it. I agreed and decided to go with him. He had been stationed there as a young brother.

We took the community car with us and drove from New York to Canada, in three days. As we left the hot "tar beaches" of El Barrio and drove north, it meant that at least three other worlds awaited us. First were the wealthy suburbs of Westchester County, New York, with tall oak and elm trees and "McMansions" owned by the New York City commercial titans. The Hutchinson River Parkway meanders through tiny, wealthy towns, with their numerous private golf courses and tennis courts bordering the Hutchinson River Parkway and its tight curves through Westchester County.

Entering New England and the Merritt Parkway in Connecticut, we were treated to more rolling hills, wealthy towns, and tons of greenery. It was refreshing to say the least. Massachusetts and Maine were not much different, except Maine had, and still has, an ambiance all to itself. On Route 95, there are signs that actually warn against crossing elk and moose, and their numerous coastline towns serve the best lobster in America. Kennebunkport, Maine, is the summer home of the Bush family, and one must drive through miles of small towns with their greenery, vegetable and fruit stands, and ice cream parlors to eventually meet up with the rocky crags of magnificent coastline that go on for miles and miles.

Maine felt like it would never end, with its popular federal and state parks inviting thousands of campers and hikers. Finally New Brunswick, Canada, approached, and we kept on driving.

One of the highlights of the trip was our introduction to Nova Scotia. I am half-Scottish, so when we saw the bagpiper welcoming us to the land of "New Scotland," I was particularly thrilled. Evidently, it is a tradition that a piper plays at the vistors' center every day to welcome tourists like ourselves. It also meant we were getting closer to North Sydney, Nova Scotia, the eastern end of the province, where we met the six-hour ferry to Newfoundland.

As we drove the trans-Canada highway across the entire island of Newfoundland, we stopped at various schools that were operated by the Christian Brothers. I enjoyed it immensely because I was reunited with some of my Canadian counterparts whom I met while in formation.

Both Frank and I found the drive from New York through New Brunswick to the coast of Nova Scotia invigorating and relaxing.

After our reunion with many Christian Brothers who had gathered for the centennial celebration, we decided to put the car on a ferry and re-connect with the United States. This time however, we took the much more relaxing 18-hour ferry from Argentia, Newfoundland, to North Sydney, Nova Scotia. It was arranged for us by a Christian Brother whose relative was a manager of the Canadian transportation agency.

I began to get a slightly uncomfortable feeling from Brother Frank while sharing a cabin on the ferry. While he never touched me, I got the feeling that he wanted us to sleep in the same bunk on the way from Newfoundland to the U.S.A. It never happened, partly because I made sure I either feigned sleep or fell asleep. But I would learn about Brother Frank's intentions a few years later.

It was 1979, and I had been sexually abused by Brother Matthew Aquinas through my time at my first school assignment and then also at my second assignment. I was also being made aware of the aberrant behavior by Brother Edwin Ignatius at Blessed Sacrament High School in New Rochelle, New York.

At Blessed Sacrament High School, I whistleblew what I saw the superior and the principal doing to the high school boys. My whistleblowing was directed to the higher ups of the Christian Brothers regarding Brother Edwin Ignatius.

For three years, I pleaded with the authorities to get rid of Brother Edwin Ignatius, who was around teenagers all the time and placed his hands on them too frequently. Nobody would listen. I kept up my protests, and in 1979, Brother Edwin Ignatius was transferred to a large archdiocesan high school, but because I was the whistleblower, I was transferred also, back to the inner city. I was glad the kids at Blessed Sacrament High School were safer now that Brother Edwin Ignatius was gone, but I worried about the kids in his new school.

Brother Edwin Ignatius eventually left the Christian Brothers and became a priest in a New England diocese.

I recall Msgr. Kenneth Lasch dropping his head after hearing more stories of abuse by Christian Brothers. He had deduced by then that our conversation was going to last a lot longer than he thought.

The summer I was transferred to Rice High School in Harlem New York (1979), the summer sabbatical period had kicked in again. I, like all the other brothers, was given a certain amount of money to do whatever I wanted to do and go wherever I wanted to go. I was feeling particularly anxious and depressed since Brother Matthew Aquinas was still abusing me, and I couldn't seem to stay away from him without risking being exposed. I didn't feel like going anywhere on vacation. I wanted to slide under a rock. That spring, I had received my master's degree in English from Manhattan College, and most of that degree was fuzzy to me. I guess I did enough to get through. I do remember loving the study of dramatic literature with a wonderful professor who also loved drama and theater. It was such a wonderful experience that I still remember the name of the late professor, Dr. Paul Cortissoz.

I decided to go home for part of my sabbatical vacation in 1979, and I only went downhill from there. I became more and more depressed, and my parents were on the verge of taking me to a hospital when I asked them to call Brother Frank, to whom I could speak and get some advice. Brother Frank had gotten a degree in psychology from Saint Bonaventure University. He was assigned at the time to a large archdiocesan high school in the city, and I thought I could trust him to hear my history of abuse.

When I finally spoke to Brother Frank, he agreed to meet me at a Burger King on Staten Island. I met him there, and we spoke for three to four hours. I finally had told someone my entire story; at least, the story I was knowledgeable about at the time. When we finished talking, I asked Brother Frank to come back to New Jersey with me to calm my parents and assure them that I would be okay. Frank had assured me during our talk that all the abuse I suffered was not my fault, that I should not feel guilty or shameful, and that those who pursued me, groomed me, and sexually abused me were the troubled persons, not I. I felt as if a thousand-pound boulder had been lifted from my shoulders.

Frank and I drove to New Jersey, and when we arrived, my parents noticed that my disposition had changed. Frank and I talked to my parents at the kitchen table for a couple of hours, and they seemed to be relieved. My parents insisted that Frank spend the night since the trip back to the city would have gotten him back there around midnight. They set up the bedroom next to mine for him. I recall that I fell asleep immediately and slept soundly for the first time in my adult life. Unfortunately, sometime during the night, I felt something or someone crawling into my bed, and I awoke, stunned and in fear. I suddenly realized that it was Brother Martin Francis Connelly, and he began to sexually abuse me in exactly the same manner others abused me, which I described to him a few hours previously. My response to seeing him was to freeze in place and utter to myself, *Oh, shit, not again.*

I awoke the next morning and said nothing to Frank or anyone else. Frank said nothing and simply had his breakfast. I had to drive him back to the city because it was my parents' car I had used to get him there. I wasn't sure what to think, but one thing I concluded was that I had told Frank at the Burger King that I was not going to allow Brother Matthew Aquinas to abuse me anymore, so he immediately gave himself permission to take Matthew Aquinas' place as a sexual abuser. I spent the remainder of the sabbatical vacation at my parents' house trying to distract myself from what Connelly had just done.

CHAPTER EIGHT

FORE! AND FOREPLAY

After sabbatical vacation, I was reporting to my new assignment, Rice High School in Harlem New York. I had been given a key to get into the building, and I let myself in. Since it was still August, some of the brothers were still on vacation, and I climbed the three stories to the main residence of the brothers. I walked through the door separating the staircase and the residence, and I heard a television playing. I walked into the television room, and there was a scary sight. The principal, Brother Louis Kelly, had stood up and was holding a shotgun. He didn't aim it at me when he realized it was me, but said he had it by his side because he was living there alone and needed protection. I couldn't believe it. My room was on the second floor, and I moved my belongings in. I quickly set up my room and got out of there. Brother Kelly had been assigned to be a principal in the inner city, but he was terrified of it to the point of needing a shotgun for protection.

I spent two years back in Harlem at Rice High School (1979–1981) and professed final vows while I was stationed there. I was a religious for life, at least I thought so then. Fortunately, my abuser, Brother Matthew Aquinas, had left the Christian Brothers around the same time. Matthew Aquinas was gone, but Brother Martin Francis Connelly had now taken his place.

As a lay person, Matthew Aquinas completed a master's degree in business and was called on by Brother Felix O'Shaughnessy, who by now had become the President of the Christian Brothers to assist with the finances of the province. Matthew Aquinas had once confided in me that he asked to see a well-known and trusted Christian Brother psychologist, Brother John Mark McDonald, a popular college professor and a professor at a major seminary.

Brother Matthew Aquinas then went for counseling, and McDonald sexually abused him during a session. McDonald, a chain smoker, died at a young age. At any rate, Matthew Aquinas was finally out of my life, for the most part, and, according to him, he had been sexually abused in religious life, too.

I asked Msgr. Kenneth Lasch if he wanted to take a break from my conversation with him, but he told me to continue. I then told him that around the same time I was transferred back to the inner city, Brother Martin Francis Connelly was transferred to upstate New York. What a relief, I thought. But Frank found ways to keep me close so he could sexually abuse me. He asked me to meet him in an upstate brothers' school for an event such as a jubilee for a brother. We were assigned separate rooms, but he came into my room in the dead of night and began sexually abusing me. I tried not to make any noise for fear we would be found out. I got through that night and spent the rest of the next day feeling ashamed and guilty.

I also made a mistake telling Brother Frank that I would love to attend the PGA event in or around 1980, which was being held at Oak Hill Country Club outside Rochester, New York. One of the major contributors to the school upstate, Bishop Carney High School, was a member of the club, and Brother Frank provided me tickets to the entire tournament. I had played the course with the school donor previously, who was a medical doctor, and I was excited to follow the professionals around the beautiful and difficult course.

Brother Frank insisted that I stay at the Christian Brothers' residence on top of Bishop Carney High School. In fact, the principal of the school was on vacation, so Brother Frank arranged that I could stay in the principal's suite of rooms, which included a bedroom, sitting room, and bathroom. The cost of getting the suite, however, was sleeping with Brother Frank during the days I was there.

I arrived at the golf course as early as I could (Connelly drove me there and dropped me off since I did not have my own car) and stayed as late as I could, not only watching the golf games, but also the practice sessions as well, which took place until dark. Needless to say, I was thrilled to be around the golf tournament, but scared to death to be around Connelly. Since there were other brothers living in the community at the time, I thought we would be found out.

For about a year and a half, Brother Martin Francis Connelly sexually abused me in my parents' New Jersey home, in Christian Brother communities in upstate New York, and several other places. I grew more anxious and depressed, but I still could not share the abuse with anyone. After all, I had spilled my guts once and gotten sexually abused as a result.

I explained to Msgr. Kenneth Lasch that I was getting to the end of the story; he simply told me to take my time. I mentioned to him that I had been transferred to Catholic Memorial High School in Boston in 1981 after two years in the city, and I was happy to be out of the New York metropolitan area. However, the demons I carried didn't go away.

The first half of 1981–82 in New England went fairly well, although I couldn't shake the anxiety and depression. I loved the kids in the New England school and tried to distract myself from the abuse by getting involved in a hundred activities. Then came Easter vacation, 1982.

Robert M. Hoatson, Ph.D.

I drove home to New Jersey during Holy Week and was counting on spending my Easter week visiting friends and perhaps playing some golf with my brothers. However, depression hit in a major way, and I could not get out of bed. My parents, once again, were concerned that I was going downhill, so they planned on getting me into a hospital. Instead, I asked them to call Martin Francis Connelly so I could speak to him. Yes, I asked one of my sexual abusers for help. I did that because my parents were under the impression he had helped me recover from the abuse episode in 1979 and so by calling him, I could at least avoid a hospital stay.

I was due back to Boston on Easter Monday, but I knew I wasn't ready to go back into a classroom. Martin Francis Connelly showed up at my parents' house on Easter Sunday and made a phone call to the headmaster in New England, telling him that I wouldn't be back until Easter Tuesday because I was anxious and depressed. The headmaster and the community superior were very compassionate and told me not to rush back. Connelly then told them that he would be driving me back to Boston on Easter Tuesday, which he did. As soon as we arrived at Catholic Memorial High School and I brought my bags to my room, Martin Francis Connelly laid me on my bed and sexually assaulted me again. I said to myself, *That's the last time you will abuse me, you son of a bitch.* And it was.

I knew I needed therapy, so I arranged with the headmaster and superior to get into therapy as soon as I returned to New England and asked for their advice as to whom I could see. The school nurse's husband was a general practitioner, and he recommended a top-notch, Harvard-educated psychiatrist. I saw the psychiatrist on Easter Tuesday, and he prescribed an anti-depressant and anti-anxiety medicine. I saw him for a number of sessions, but he terminated our sessions after a few months. He told me he didn't think there was much wrong with me. That shocked me at first, but then I realized he was right; there was nothing wrong with *me*, but there was a lot wrong with those who sexually abused me. I was unable to tell him about other abusive situations because my memory had not yet returned and would not return for many years.

Unfortunately, one of the Christian Brothers, a gossip par excellence, spread the word among the Catholic Memorial High School faculty and staff that I had had a nervous breakdown, yet he never offered me a fraternal word of support. I surmised that it was just because I had previously defeated him in an election for membership on the community leadership team, and he never was able to shake the fact of that defeat. He died at a fairly young age.

"Well, Father Ken, that's the end of my story of sexual abuse. Thanks for listening," I said. Father Ken expressed his sorrow and empathy and was very happy I had left the Christian Brothers after all that abuse. He wondered why I became a priest after all that, and I told him that I thought the diocesan priesthood would allow me to live a more independent life. I wouldn't have to live in communities of men, and perhaps I would be safer. Father Ken then expressed his opinion that we needed to stop for the time being, but that he was open to talking further.

Robert M. Hoatson, Ph.D.

CHAPTER NINE

MY NON-PROFIT AND TROUBLE WITH ARCHBISHOP JOHN J. MYERS

Before I left, I told Msgr. Kenneth Lasch about my plans to start a non-profit charity to help victim/survivors and that my therapist was very enthusiastic about it. I mentioned to Father Ken that I thought the granddaddy of clergy sexual abuse advocacy organizations, SNAP (Survivors Network of Those Abused by Priests), founded in 1989, was doing superb work, but it wasn't giving direct help to victims, like my two former students, Bobby and Sean. I felt that there was a growing need for an organization that would advocate for victims but also provide food, clothing, shelter, and other essential needs to victims.

Father Ken agreed wholeheartedly and admitted that he had spoken to the leaders of SNAP with a similar idea. He and I loved that organization but thought its public advocacy was not enough. He felt victims needed direct services, so I asked Ken if he would join me in co-founding a non-profit organization. He said yes, and I continued my plan to start a non-profit charity in New Jersey.

Having spoken to Msgr. Kenneth Lasch to finally reveal my story as I knew it at the time, I returned to Our Lady of Good Counsel Parish to continue to lead the two schools and help them get on a more solid footing. I had gotten into some trouble with the archbishop, John J. Myers, a roly-poly, red-faced cleric who came to Newark from the Midwest, because one of his first actions as archbishop was to ban eulogies by lay people at funerals.

It did not surprise me that Archbishop Myers would pull some stunt when he arrived because his reputation preceded him. When he was in the Midwest, he acted dictatorial, and I followed his tenure there through the Catholic media. For example, he was anti-gay, and if and when a Catholic teacher or other employee "came out of the closet," he had them fired. In addition, he was recruiting large classes of men for ordination for his diocese. He was garnering favor with the pope, who loved bishops who ordained lots of priests. He and Archbishop Theodore McCarrick, who ordained me, were in competition for the most ordinations each year.

When Myers banned eulogies by lay persons at funerals, I wrote to him and objected strenuously. My letter claimed that eulogies by lay people at funerals were one of the most powerful liturgical practices the Church had allowed. Lay people loved the eulogies by family members or friends, and it gave families and acquaintances a wonderful way to grieve. Myers did not like my letter and responded by saying that I was the only priest who objected to this decree. I followed my letter to him with a letter to the editor of a national Catholic newspaper, which covered the story of Myers banning eulogies.

My letter to the newspaper was published in February, 2002. It talked about a real-life experience I had with a family from a Bergen County, New Jersey, parish. A woman named Mrs. Dorothy Finnegan died. She was a long-time parishioner, and she and her husband raised their family in the parish. Her children were very successful. Two of her sons became federal law enforcement agents, and one of them, Jack Finnegan, was the agent who protected Pope John Paul II from the time his plane landed in the United States to the time his plane left for Italy, including the pope's visit to Sacred Heart Cathedral Basilica and the Mass he celebrated in Giants' Stadium in 1995.

I was asked to preside at the funeral of Mrs. Finnegan at the parish church, but I had to inform the family that the eulogy by a family member would have to take place in the funeral home the night before. Jack Finnegan eulogized his mother brilliantly, but it would have been much more effective in the parish church where his mother worshiped for decades. My letter to the editor indicated that it was okay for Jack Finnegan to stand beside or behind the pope every step of his visit to the United States, risking his life to protect the pope, even entering sanctuaries in Cathedrals and churches to be as close to the pope as possible. But he was not allowed to enter his family's parish sanctuary to eulogize his mother.

Needless to say, Archbishop Myers was not happy with my letter and the criticism of his eulogy ban. I expected a retaliation or a discipline, but nothing came immediately. However, assistant superintendent of archdiocesan elementary schools, Sister Mary Agnes Smith, came for a visit to the elementary school in March or April, 2003, and confided in the principal, Pat McGrath, that Myers had plans to fire me and that it might be soon. Mrs. McGrath warned me, but I was not surprised. Sister Mary Agnes Smith was a Sister of St. Joseph from New York and was a straight shooter.

I was not surprised that Sister Mary Agnes brought that information to the school that day because I sensed that Archbishop Myers had to do something to try to shut me up and get me under control. Since I had told my story to Father Ken Lasch months earlier, I was getting more courageous about my own story of abuse and the stories of my fellow victim/survivors. I attended a meeting at St. Thomas More Parish in Manalapan, NJ on a Saturday morning around March, 2002, at which the Attorney General spoke about clergy sexual abuse and his efforts to hold the Catholic Church accountable for covering it up.

The parish was led by Father John Bambrick, a native of New Jersey and a victim/survivor of sexual abuse by Father Anthony Eremito of the New York Archdiocese. Father John Bambrick got involved in the victim/survivor movement in the early 1990s and was heavily involved as a leader of a victims' organization. Eremito, who was stationed at a parish in New York, met John Bambrick at a parish in central New Jersey, where John was the teenage sacristan. Father Anthony Eremito went to John's parish one weekend to perform a wedding and befriended John. He then began to sexually abuse him. When John reported the abuse to Church officials, he ran into a morally compromised group of leaders but refused to back down. He remains a pastor today.

The meeting at St. Thomas was the first meeting of victim/survivors and advocates I had ever attended. Father John Bambrick was very welcoming as were other local survivor leaders. They congratulated me for coming and speaking at the meeting. Shaking, I stood up and told the group I had just moved out of a rectory in Essex County, New Jersey, because a pedophile priest was moved in. The crowd applauded me. Father Joseph Petrillo, the pastor of Our Lady of Lourdes Parish, had moved his best friend, Monsignor Peter Cheplic, into the rectory of Our Lady of Lourdes Parish because he had been removed as a pastor in Hudson County when he admitted to sexually abusing a child in the 1970s.

Sitting next to me at the meeting was a reporter for the local newspaper, who quoted me publicly for the first time about my moving out of the rectory.

CHAPTER TEN

ONE PEDO MOVING IN, ME MOVING OUT

How is it that I moved out of the rectory of Our Lady of Lourdes Parish in my hometown of West Orange, New Jersey? One day after I returned to the rectory from school, Father Joseph Petrillo asked to see me in my room and told me he was going to allow Monsignor Peter Cheplic to move in. I told Joseph that he couldn't move Peter into our rectory because a credibly accused priest was not allowed to live in church quarters. Joseph then said to me, "Bob, the least we can do for a brother is give him safe haven." I reminded him that the parish had an elementary school about two hundred yards from the bedroom where Peter Cheplic would be living. I emphasized that we could not put those children at risk. Joseph assured me that Peter assured him that he had only abused a child once and he had never done it again. It turned out that Peter Cheplic had more than one victim, and one young man had been abused by him for years.

When Father Joseph Petrillo left my room that evening, I had a serious anxiety attack. Father Petrillo was going to move a pedophile into my rectory, and he would be living across the hall from me. I ended up with a serious case of gastritis, causing me to go to an emergency room for treatment. I also had a therapy appointment with my therapist, and I expressed my desire to move out of that rectory. He agreed wholeheartedly that I should move out. I felt better immediately.

I made an appointment with the Vicar General of the Archdiocese, Bishop Arthur Serratelli, and met him in his office in Newark. I informed him that Father Joseph Petrillo, by that time, had moved Monsignor Peter Cheplic into the rectory of Our Lady of Lourdes and that I did not approve of that. Bishop Serratelli then said of

Monsignor Cheplic, "That poor man, what he's been through." I was shocked that Bishop Serratelli would take the side of the pedophile priest but quickly learned that that was the modus operandi of the Church; namely, to protect the image and the assets of the Church, including its pedophile clergy, and to ignore the victim/survivors. He then engaged me in some conversation about my knowledge of clergy sexual abuse as if he were interested in really learning about it. I gave him some tips, but he clearly wasn't interested.

Since I told Bishop Serratelli I wouldn't live in a rectory with a pedophile priest, he told me to move out and find a rectory to live in. Since I was serving on weekends at a Bergen County parish, I thought maybe I could move in there. Actually, the vice principal of Our Lady of Good Counsel High School, Mr. Andrew Van Houten, lived in the rectory of the parish and told me there was plenty of room there for me.

Andrew Van Houten had been hired as vice principal of Our Lady of Good Counsel High School just as I was being named Director of Schools in approximately June, 2001. When I was told by the principal, Mrs. Gladys Ramos, that she had hired Mr. Van Houten, I knew immediately to whom she was referring. Andrew Van Houten had been a Christian Brother with me for many years. He taught and was an administrator, including being principal, at several Catholic and private schools. I was happy to know that I would be reunited in ministry with someone who had plenty of educational experience.

Mr. Van Houten recommended that I speak to Father Dan O'Herlihy, the pastor of the parish, and ask him if there was a room for me. Mr. Van Houten lived at St. Timothy's rectory in Bergen County, New Jersey, because he was the director of religious education for the parish while he was a Christian Brother, but shortly after, he took a leave of absence from the Christian Brothers. I spoke to Father Dan, and he welcomed me to St. Timothy's rectory around June, 2002. My quarters were very comfortable and adequate. I was able to say early morning Mass for the nuns who lived in the convent next door before I left for school in Newark. The trip to Newark took at least forty-five minutes.

By the time I moved into St. Timothy's Parish, my reputation as an advocate for victim/survivors was growing. I appeared on Boston media a few times after I started helping my former students, Bobby and Sean. I met their attorney, Mitchell Garabedian, around that time. Attorney Garabedian deposed me in the cases of Bobby and Sean, and I believe I was helpful in attaining the financial settlements that the archdiocese gave each of them.

Shortly after I moved into St. Timothy's rectory, I was asked by one of the parish nuns if I was the priest who was helping victims in sexual abuse cases. I answered, "Yes, I am." She then asked to see me.

I met her in the front parlor of the rectory, and she recounted a story of how abusive the sister superior was in the convent. There was no sexual abuse, but every other form, including psychological abuse, was described. The sister was too fearful to report her to her religious superiors, so I did. Father Dan O'Herlihy, pastor, caught on that one nun after another was coming to see me in the front parlor of the rectory to report the abuse by the sister superior. Father Dan and the sister superior were two peas in a pod and got along famously. Both were abusive in many ways, and I soon realized that I would have to escape from that rectory, too.

Father Dan began to cut back my Mass schedule, gave my garage to the sister superior, and admonished me for not putting the Sunday newspaper sections back in order after I read them. The nuns continued to see me, and the more they saw me, the worse it got for me in the rectory. Father Dan was surrounded by sycophants who reported everything to him, and if he didn't like what he heard, he lost his temper. Father Dan knew all about the nuns coming to see me. The climate in the rectory deteriorated to the point that I stopped eating there.

Around December, 2002, while Father Dan was on his day off, I borrowed my father's pick-up truck and moved myself out of St. Timothy's rectory. I moved into the apartment at Our Lady of Good Counsel rectory that had been built for the lay principal, who could use the apartment if he had to stay late for meetings and other events. I never returned to St. Timothy's. My letters to the superiors of the nuns were answered with, "Mind your own business." Consequently, I reported the abusive nun to the vicar for religious of the archdiocese, a religious sister who was the liaison between the archdiocese and members of religious orders. She didn't do anything to rectify the matter, and neither did the vicar for priests, whom I had reached out to for help.

Fortunately, shortly after I was ordained in 1997, Dr. Geraldine Chapey, former dean of the School of Education at St. John's University, where I was the assistant dean, had offered me the use of a studio apartment overlooking the Atlantic Ocean. She said I would need some place to go on my days off. She lived on the ninth floor of a high-rise on the ocean, and the studio was just down the hall. Dr. Chapey, a red-headed Irishwoman through and through, had hired me in 1989 to take over for her as assistant dean for undergraduate education at St. John's. She was named dean of the entire school at that time. That studio apartment became my refuge from the insanity, retaliation, and harassment from the archdiocese, and I began to commute from the studio apartment to New Jersey in order to preserve my sanity, which was being seriously tested by a corrupt archdiocese. The studio apartment on the ninth floor overlooking the Atlantic Ocean was my oasis.

CHAPTER ELEVEN

SENATE HEARING TESTIMONY AND MY SUBSEQUENT FIRING

In May, 2003, a New York State Senator announced a hearing regarding possible changes in the statutes of limitations on childhood sexual abuse allegations in New York State. By that time, I had come to know many activists in the victim/survivor movement, and they encouraged me to attend. It was Tuesday, May 20, 2003, and I headed to Albany for the hearing. As I sat listening to at least eight hours of testimony, I decided to put my name on the list of those who would speak. It wasn't until 5:30 p.m. or so that my name was called by Senator Tom Duane. Much of the crowd had left, but Catholic Church lobbyists and authorities stayed for my testimony, including executives of the New York State Catholic Conference, the lobby arm of the New York bishops.

Senator Tom Duane, who represented Manhattan for years, was most respectful and attentive despite the many hours of testimony, much of which was too long, but there was no time limit attached to the testimony. Wearing my black suit and collar, I walked to the front of the hearing room, sat at the table where a microphone was located, and began my comments. I had jotted down what I wanted to say as I listened to so many others. My most controversial comment called for the resignation of any bishop in the United States who had covered up the sexual abuse of children.

By the time I testified, there were only two senators left; namely, Tom Duane and Senator Liz Kruger, who also represented parts of Manhattan. She thanked me profusely for my testimony and said I was a courageous priest for saying what I said about the bishops. However, I was told later that evening that members of the New York Catholic Conference quickly left their seats and headed for the exits to use their cell phones as soon as I made the comment about the bishops. Some of my fellow advocates thought they were angry at what I said and didn't want to listen any longer, but something else was brewing.

When I returned to work at Our Lady of Good Counsel Schools on Wednesday, a day after the hearing, I received a telephone call from the secretary of Vicar General, Bishop Arthur Serratelli. She asked me to be in Archbishop Myers' office on Friday in the morning. I knew I was in trouble. I arrived on Friday and was asked to go to the second floor where the corporate headquarters were located. I arrived on the second floor and was met by an ornery secretary and was instructed to sit in a waiting room. I knew the archbishop's office was to the left of this waiting room, so I thought I would be summoned to enter his office soon.

Instead, the door behind me opened up, and Bishop Arthur Serratelli was sitting alone at a large conference table that could seat about a dozen people at least. In the corner of the room sat Father Francis Moriarty, one of Archbishop Myers' favorites, who was ordained two years after me but was tagged by Myers as one of his "special assistants." Father Francis Moriarty was either studying for his degree in canon law or had finished it. It was very strange to sit across from Bishop Serratelli and have Father Moriarty sitting in the corner of the same room like a robot. Father Moriarty and I were actually fairly friendly in the seminary. He and I were in the seminary choir as well. He died at a young age.

Bishop Serratelli greeted me and then began. He told me that officials of the Albany Diocese had telephoned Archbishop Myers and told him that I had used some inflammatory language during my testimony before the Senate subcommittee. He then reminded me that I owed obedience to the archbishop, that I needed to tone down my language, and that I had to watch what I said in public about bishops. Then, he slid an envelope across the table at me and asked me to open it.

The envelope contained a letter from Archbishop Myers indicating that I was fired as Director of Schools at Our Lady of Good Counsel Parish because there were complaints about me from members of the board of directors, a made-up excuse. The firing was effective immediately, according to the letter from Archbishop Myers, but Bishop Serratelli then said, "You have to stay at the schools until after both graduations." He then asked me to cooperate fully with my replacement. Father Peter Page, pastor of two parishes in Union County, was tapped to replace me. Although I was fired as Director of Schools, my priesthood was not taken from me. I was able to say Mass and administer the sacraments.

I did stay until June, and I enjoyed every minute of it. The principals were worried about my replacement, Father Peter Page, who had an interesting occupation before becoming a priest, because he did not have a good reputation from the schools and parishes in which he had previously worked. Graduations in June went smoothly, but a humorous story about the high school graduation must be told. Sister Joan Ruth Whittle was in charge of the graduation ceremony for the high school, and on the night of graduation, no one was allowed into the church without a ticket because of seating limitations. Sister Joan Ruth was monitoring the main door of the church when a man showed up without a ticket.

Sister Joan Ruth asked him where his ticket was, and he responded, "I am Joseph Devine from the archdiocese." Sister Joan Ruth welcomed him and then talked about how badly I was being treated by the archdiocese. She then said, "Do you ever live up to your last name?" Mr. Devine responded, "Many people don't think so." He then sat in the wings of the church to spy on my talk to the graduates, as if I would include any of my issues in a graduation talk that was meant for our seniors and eighth graders. He was sent by Bishop Serratelli, no doubt. Serratelli's politics as vicar general were rewarded with him being named the bishop of a diocese in New Jersey. He stayed there for a long time, and the skeletons in his closet would become a source of interesting conversation in his diocese for his entire time there.

Following graduations, I completed the school year with the two principals and wandered the archdiocese for nearly a year. Since I hadn't had a vacation in nearly four years, I asked Bishop Serratelli for a couple months' vacation, and he agreed to it. I was still the weekend assistant pastor in two parishes in Bergen County because Archbishop Myers did not remove my faculties to function as a priest; he simply fired me from Our Lady of Good Counsel Schools, so I had time off except for the weekends.

I enjoyed both parishes very much, and the pastor of one of the parishes was particularly supportive of my work with clergy abuse victims. Some of the parishioners weren't happy with a couple of my homilies regarding the sexual abuse crisis, but the pastor did not bend to their complaints. He consistently said that the clergy abuse crisis had to be dealt with and resolved.

I spent those last two months still living at Our Lady of Good Counsel Schools and had no idea what would follow after that. The Archdiocese of Newark refused to give me an assignment. The pastor of the second parish, Father Joe Fitzpatrick, with whom I was very friendly at one time, evidently received a phone call from Bishop Serratelli who told Father Joe that I was going to live at Father Joe's parish, Nativity, in Midland Park, New Jersey, so he could monitor and spy on me. There was a house next to the rectory that was once a convent, and Monsignor Frederick Dickerson, a retired priest, lived on the entire first floor. The second floor was in the midst of being renovated, but it in no way was finished, except for two tiny rooms (they looked just like the cells the nuns would have used as bedrooms) that were painted and carpeted. There was a bathroom off one of the rooms, but that was tiny, too. They were the rooms in which Father Joe Fitzpatrick told me I would be living.

My bed extended from one wall to the other in the supposed bedroom. I could not pass in front of the bed to get to the bedroom window. I had to pass over the bed to get to the other side of the room. My sitting room was barely large enough for one chair and a television. I decided not to make a big scene since I knew I would be living out of the studio in Rockaway Beach, New York soon, anyway. I moved most of my belongings to Rockaway Beach and pretended, at times, to be living in the rooms I was assigned. I always signed "out" for dinner, so I never ate in that rectory. I basically was on my own. Fortunately, I continued to receive my salary, which was mandated by canon law.

Father Joe Fitzpatrick became the priest who reported my comings and goings to Bishop Serratelli. They didn't know what to do with me.

As mentioned earlier, my successor at Our Lady of Good Counsel Schools was Father Peter Page, and the two principals, Pat McGrath and Harry Hart, had heard disturbing information about Father Page's history in other schools in particular. He was proud of his culinary talents and bragged once that he invited the parish kids in to share dinners with him. I asked the person who told me that, "What? Has anyone told the archbishop that he has kids in the rectory?" The person who told me said, "What's wrong with a priest cooking for the kids of his parish?" "Duh," I responded, "there aren't supposed to be any kids in a rectory without their parents or other adult supervision."

As that summer of 2003 proceeded, and I finished up at Our Lady of Good Counsel Schools, my replacement, Father Peter Page, met with the two principals but ignored me completely. I didn't mind. I knew Peter Page wouldn't last very long. Within four months, he was removed as Director of Schools. He was accused of inappropriately touching an eighth-grade boy, the same boy who, as an elementary student in a neighboring Catholic elementary school, had been inappropriately touched by another priest, Father Leslie

Harcourt, whom the diocese transferred after the event. Without having told me or principal Pat McGrath about the encounter that Jonathan had at the other school, Jonathan had come to us as a seventh-grader, and we found out through the grapevine what had happened to him.

Mrs. McGrath and I had talked about Jonathan and promised that we would take care of him. Jonathan had begun to feel very comfortable around Mrs. McGrath and me, and she and I would greet him every morning with a "Good morning, Jonathan" because he arrived two minutes before the late bell rang. He even started to smile when he arrived at school. Jonathan was beginning to trust adults again, especially priests like myself. He was a great kid who got along with the other kids and was like any other teenaged boy.

Approximately two months into the 2003–2004 school year, I was driving back to Rockaway Beach one afternoon when I received a telephone call. "Hello," I said, "This is Father Bob," while the voice on the other end said, "This is Pat McGrath." "Hi, Pat," I said, "How are you doing?" She said, "I need to speak to you about something serious," and I, of course, said, "Go ahead, Pat."

"Father Bob, I have received a complaint against Father Peter Page. He allegedly has been touching Jonathan in the cafeteria, and Jonathan is feeling very uneasy. He seems to go behind Jonathan, grab his collar and sweater in an affectionate manner, and make comments to him." I said, "Oh, my God, not again." Pat then said, "I think I know what to do, but I want to check with you."

Mrs. McGrath's phone call came as I drove from New Jersey to Rockaway Beach, and I had her on speaker phone. I was coming from a doctor's office in New Jersey, where I was told that I had a serious kidney disease, C1Q Nephropathy, which my nephrologist labeled a children's disease. He said he usually sees perhaps three or four adults annually who have the disease. I was dealing with that news when I told Mrs. McGrath, "Pat, call the police and then follow the archdiocesan policies." She was hesitant to call the police because she wasn't positive that what happened would have been considered sexual abuse of a child. I went back and forth with her for a few minutes about the phone call to the police because I was of the mind that who knows how far Father Peter Page went with his touching? Did he pull heavily on Jonathan's collar and feel his back? Did he give him a back rub? Did he go around his body and touch any other body parts like his chest? Anything else? Mrs. McGrath believed it stopped at the collar and neck.

At the time, the person in the archdiocese who received reports of clergy sexual abuse was one and the same Joseph Devine who had spied on me at graduation, and was still the Director of Communications. This was done deliberately, in my opinion, so that when claims of clergy sexual abuse were reported, they could be spun immediately in favor of the priest and the archdiocese.

Mrs. McGrath spoke to Mr. Devine and archdiocesan school officials, and she was told that it would be taken care of. The next day, Father Peter Page was removed from Our Lady of Good Counsel Schools, and he was allowed to remain as pastor of his two parishes. I must admit I gloated for a time, but I was worried about Jonathan because this was now his second time being touched inappropriately by a priest. Because of the motherly and professional care of Mrs. McGrath, Jonathan stayed the rest of the year and graduated from Our Lady of Good Counsel Elementary School.

Father Page has supposedly retired from both of the parishes of which he was in charge.

Robert M. Hoatson, Ph.D.

CHAPTER TWELVE

ASSISTING VICTIMS AND HELPING MYSELF HEAL

From June, 2003, until January, 2004, I was without a full-time assignment as a priest, so I lived in the studio apartment in Rockaway Beach. It was like I had died and gone to heaven. I had brought most of my belongings to my parents' garage in eastern New Jersey and lived very simply in the studio with my computer equipment, which quickly became the headquarters of our non-profit charity.

The original name we chose for the non-profit was Rescue and Recovery International, but those interested in our ministry, who became members of our first board of directors, thought that name was not adequate, so we changed our charity's name to a more simplified version, which actually came from one of our long-time volunteers, Ernest Barbato, who lives in the South. He recommended the new name, Road to Recovery, Inc., on a phone call one evening.

Our final incorporation as a non-profit charity occurred in 2005. A parishioner of one of the parishes in which I served who was also a financial expert recommended an attorney who does legal work for establishing non-profit corporations. We are forever indebted to the law firm and its attorneys for their pro-bono work in getting our non-profit charity registered legally with the state of New Jersey and the federal government.

A member of one of the parishes where I was stationed for three years (1998–2001), Anthony W. Vasile, CPA, was a well-known and respected accountant in the Bergen County area. He was and still is a member of the parish's finance committee, and he has done my taxes from 1998 until the present time. Anthony has never charged any priest a fee for completing their taxes each year. He expressed interest in helping our charity with its accounting needs, and he has been our pro-bono accountant and financial expert since our founding, to the present. His partner, Michele Fronduto, CPA, makes up the other half of the accounting firm that serves us so well. They have been invaluable contributors to the work of our non-profit charity.

The non-profit began to collect tax-free donations to help victim/survivors, and all of our donations at that time went to help me travel to many parts of the country, especially New England, since many victims began to call looking for help. Most of our "clients" learned about us from our initial website and word of mouth. The calls came in by the dozen weekly, and it was not unusual for my cars to have 200,000 miles on them within a couple of years. I loved what I was doing, and I knew that God was calling me to assist clergy sexual abuse victims and their families. I loved being able to tell a victim, "I am so sorry for what happened to you," and "You did nothing wrong," and "How can we help you recover?"

At the same time, I began to work with attorneys, advocates, and therapists. My first bit of advice to victims was to get into therapy. My experience taught me that therapy was the key to survival, and our charity began to help pay for therapy sessions for victims. The second bit of advice concerned their personal needs. "Do you have a place to live?" "Do you have regular meals?" and "Do you have decent clothes to wear?" Not surprisingly, many answered, "No, I don't." I recall bringing victims to hotels and motels and paying for rooms for weeks at a time. During their weeks in the hotels and motels, I helped the victims connect with social services, welfare, and Medicaid/Medicare. I spent many hours in social security offices and welfare agencies.

Within a few days of my firing from Our Lady of Good Counsel Schools because I had called for the resignation of bishops who covered up sexual abuse, news spread throughout the country that Archbishop Myers had actually fired one of his own.

I was sitting in my office one day when the telephone rang. There was a male voice on the other end, and he said, "Father Bob, my name is Father Patrick W. Collins, and I am calling from out of state. I am a retired priest from the diocese where Archbishop Myers used to rule, Peoria, Illinois, and I just want you to know that the horrendous history of John J. Myers will be revealed before long, and you shouldn't worry. As soon as Myers became bishop in the Midwest, I fled my diocese and went to teach and preach outside the diocese because I refused to work with him. He covered up a number of sexual abuse cases, and they will become public someday." I thanked Father Collins for his supportive telephone call, and I said receiving a call from a priest was very helpful.

Father Collins then told me that there was a family in his former diocese whose son was sexually abused by a priest. The family reported the abuse to then-Bishop Myers, and Myers threatened the family with loss of their family businesses if they did not back down and stop accusing the priest. I asked Father Collins if he could put me in touch with that family, and he agreed.

Within hours, I was speaking with Helen Rainforth, a woman who, with her husband, owned two variety stores, one in the city and one in the country. She told me that Bishop Myers threatened them with legal action and that he would own their two stores if they continued to complain about one of his priests. Their son, Lance, was sexually abused at their parish, and other boys were as well, three from one family. Helen told me to stay strong and stand up to Myers, whom she described as evil. The telephone calls from Father Collins and Mrs. Rainforth boosted my spirits and convinced me that I was on the right track with Road to Recovery, Inc.

By now, it was early in 2003, and I was in my spiritual glory founding a non-profit charity and getting more and more phone calls from victims. I knew that God had planned that I should work with victims, so I wrote an official letter to Archbishop

Myers asking that my full-time ministry be to those who had been sexually abused by clergy. I reminded him that he could have a model program among the bishops of the United States for treating victims. Needless to say, he wrote back and issued a definitive, "No, you may not run a non-profit organization to help victims of sexual abuse." I then wrote back and reminded him that canon 215 of the Catholic Church's Code of Canon Law expressly permits the establishment of acts of charity and associations to help those in need. It reads, "The Christian faithful are at liberty freely to found and to govern associations for charitable and religious purposes or for the promotion of the Christian vocation in the world; they are free to hold meetings to pursue these purposes in common."

Msgr. Kenneth Lasch and I agreed that we were in communion with the church in founding our charitable organization. What greater act of charity is there than helping someone regain their life? As mental health experts agree, childhood sexual abuse is considered murder of the soul. Our charity was founded to help murdered souls to regain a sense of life and hope. Archbishop Myers never bent, so Msgr. Kenneth Lasch and I continued our work, since we believed that we were encouraged by canon law to administer a charity. Once we announced the founding of the non-profit, the phones rang off the hook. Since 2003, we estimate that 5,000+ victim/survivors and their families have been helped by this non-profit.

It wasn't long before my car was accumulating thousands of miles on its odometer. I retired one car at 300,000 miles and another at 250,000 miles. I was traveling all over the country to assist victims and their families. Anthony W. Vasile, CPA, our pro-bono accountant and donor, gave us the go-ahead to begin to collect tax-deductible donations. Believe it or not, we were collecting enough money, even at the beginning, to help some victims with food, clothing, and shelter. Father Ken never took a salary, and I did not take a salary until 2011 when I was voluntarily laicized by the Vatican. Up to then, I relied on my archdiocesan salary and benefits, which Archbishop Myers began to reduce around 2010. According to canon law, a bishop is required to support his priests despite their status, unless the priest is engaging in unlawful activities or until he officially leaves the priesthood.

I once described Archbishop Myers to the auxiliary bishops of Newark in a letter I sent them as a "malignant narcissist," and I asked them to petition the Vatican to remove him. Pope Francis must have picked up on something wrong because in 2016, he appointed a co-adjutor archbishop, Bernard Hebda, who, by canon law, had the same rank as Archbishop Myers and probably was chosen to replace him when he either reached 75 years of age, resigned, or was removed. That bishop did not last long, as he was tapped to replace a troubled bishop in the Midwest. That bishop did not assist victims to any great degree because, as he clearly stated, he worked for Archbishop Myers.

In January, 2005, I received a telephone call from Father Richard Birmingham, who was the director of clergy personnel and former secretary to Archbishop McCarrick. Father Richard asked me if I would be interested in taking a position as the chaplain of Catholic Charities and Health and Hospitals. "Bob, you would be the first chaplain of Catholic Charities and Health and Hospitals ever, and you would be able, in that position, to do your work with clergy sexual abuse victims," he told me. He asked me to meet with Salvatore Di Chiara, a leader of the health and hospital organization. I met Salvatore in his office in a suburban town, and he gave me the same pitch. I told him, "I will take the position as long it allows me to continue my work with clergy sexual abuse victims." He agreed, so I took the job.

That same year, 2005, Father Richard Birmingham was selected by Archbishop Myers to become a monsignor. However, Father Birmingham turned down the offer and wrote a letter to many of his friends and acquaintances indicating that he had turned down the offer because he had an incurable illness as a result of having lived an alternative lifestyle for years.

He was then assigned to be the driver for Bishop Felipe Diaz, and Archbishop Myers made a deal with another bishop of a New Jersey diocese to allow Father Birmingham to say Sunday Mass in a parish in that diocese in order to hide his illness and lifestyle admission. Recently, the current archbishop, Cardinal Joseph Tobin, allowed Father Birmingham to retire from the priesthood well before retirement age, and it is believed that Father Birmingham is receiving financial support from the archdiocese. Perhaps Father Birmingham will also be allowed to continue to attend the support group for priests with his illness, as allegedly, it has a sizable membership.

My Catholic Charities and Health and Hospitals office was located in a partly boarded-up building in a rundown part of the city. There were approximately twenty persons based in that building, including one of the finest women I have ever met, Catherine L'Insalata, a former nun who, for nearly forty years, was a division director of Catholic Charities and Health and Hospitals. Catherine and her staff, who ran many of the archdiocesan social services, such as food distribution, were the salt of the earth. Catherine knew the lay of the land, and she and I spoke often about the state of affairs in the archdiocese, especially concerning clergy sexual abuse. The building had a small chapel, and I presided at Mass whenever I was in the office. I visited the facilities of Catholic Charities and Health and Hospitals throughout the four counties of the archdiocese, including senior citizen centers, homeless shelters, and medical centers. I also continued to respond to clergy sexual abuse victims.

As 2005 progressed, my kidneys were still not in good health. My nephrologist prescribed a kidney biopsy, which was conducted, and my C1Q was confirmed. However, my doctor recommended that I make an appointment with a national expert in the disease who was located at a hospital in New York City. The expert nephrologist concurred with the results of the biopsy and asked me to work with my regular nephrologist to develop a treatment plan. It was explained to me that there were two main protocols to treat the disease initially: the drug Prednisone or a chemotherapy medication. He settled on Prednisone, and I was taking large doses of Prednisone every other day for several months. Thank goodness I had so much work to do because the side effects of the Prednisone were not easy to handle. Prednisone is a miracle drug, but its side effects can be daunting. It gave me more energy than I knew what to do with, and I often stayed up many nights cleaning my apartment or working on the computer.

After many months of Prednisone, my creatinine levels began to decrease—a good sign. The nephrologist put me on blood pressure medicine and another medicine to assist the kidneys, and my body responded positively. After six or seven years, he declared my kidney disease to be in remission. During the time of my diagnosis and treatment for a kidney disease that often leads to kidney failure and a transplant, I decided to retain an attorney to sue several entities because of my firing in 2003 and the sexual abuse I endured in the Christian Brothers.

My lawsuit named Cardinal Edward Egan and his archdiocese for not following up on my complaint of sexual abuse against Father Martin Francis Connelly when he was a Christian Brother; Archbishop John J. Myers and his archdiocese for firing me from my position at Our Lady of Good Counsel Schools; the Christian Brothers for not acting on my complaints against Brother Giordano, Brother Matthew Aquinas, and Brother Martin Francis Connelly; a diocese, Albany, in upstate New York, which reported my comments to Archbishop Myers while I testified at a sexual abuse hearing; and the individuals Brother Giordano, Brother Felix O'Shaughnessy, Brother Matthew Aquinas, and Brother Martin Francis Connelly, who, by that time, had become *Father* Martin Francis Connelly.

Sometime that fall, I was called to the offices of the archdiocese by officials of the hospitals and charities division. Jack O'Leary was the director, and he and Father Richard Birmingham attended, as did Monsignor Felipe Diaz, who had a position with the hospitals. I also believe Salvatore Di Chiara was in attendance. I was called on the carpet for working with clergy sexual abuse victims and not fulfilling my role as chaplain of Catholic Charities and Health and Hospitals. I reminded the group that Father Richard Birmingham and Salvatore Di Chiara offered me the job because I could and would continue my work with clergy sexual abuse victims. They acknowledged giving me permission to do that work, but they thought I would have come up with a plan of action to present to them, which they never asked for or put in my job description. I was not fooled by this meeting and suspected it had emanated from the archbishop's and vicar general's offices in order to keep the clergy sexual abuse scandal covered up.

I did not put up much of a fight because I knew I was going to file a lawsuit toward the end of the year. The group that was gathered there told me that I was to be placed under the supervision of Monsignor Felipe Diaz, who would later become *Bishop* Felipe Diaz. Felipe, as he was and is called by the clergy, had a very close friend in the archdiocese, Father George Miller. It was well-known that Bishop Diaz and Father Miller were "close" friends. Miller, no doubt with the recommendation of Bishop Diaz, was named an auxiliary bishop of Newark in 2020. Bishop Felipe Diaz, who was famous for having a collection of religious tchotchkes, including nun dolls, now had his close friend in the hierarchy. In any case, it did not matter to whom I was to report because I knew I wouldn't be assigned to anyone at all after I filed my lawsuit.

CHAPTER THIRTEEN

MY LAWSUIT AND SUBSEQUENT SUSPENSION

On December 13, 2005, I filed a RICO lawsuit in federal court in New York against all the parties named previously. RICO stands for Racketeer Influenced and Corrupt Organization Act. If there is a more deserving organization to be accused of racketeering and corruption, it is the Catholic Church. My lawsuit outlined how the church and its leaders conspired to destroy my rights as a citizen of the United States. During the process of writing up my lawsuit, much of which I did myself, I was concerned that someone would try to sue me for mentioning their names in the lawsuit. However, my attorney informed me that as long as an allegation is in a lawsuit, the person or persons mentioned cannot sue. That's all I needed to hear.

My lawsuit included allegations of sexual abuse, financial mismanagement, homosexual affairs among priests and Christian Brothers, and many other examples of clerical misconduct. Federal Judge Patrick Moore was assigned my case. He was a graduate of a Catholic university, as was his brother, who was president of the Lawyers Catholic Action club of the Archdiocese of New York. In addition, Judge Moore's wife was involved in the possible sale of a Catholic parish church nearby.

When we first appeared before Judge Moore, he actually had the nerve to say in open court to my attorney and me, "Hasn't the Church suffered enough?" My attorney then asked him, "Judge Moore, is there any reason why we might have to ask you to recuse yourself?" The judge's face turned blood red, and he retorted angrily, "No, why?" My attorney gave him some possible reasons for his recusal, including some connections my attorney's family had to judges in New York State.

Both my attorney and I then decided to ask for a formal recusal of Judge Moore, citing the fact that he admitted to attending meetings of the Catholic lawyers' organization that his brother led, and he admitted meeting Cardinal Edward Egan on more than one occasion because we were also suing Cardinal Egan. We also asked him to recuse himself because of his wife's connection with the possible sale of the aforementioned parish church, the judge admitting to attending at least one candlelight service in an attempt to save that church from being sold. His connection to a prominent Catholic university, and his question in open court, "Hasn't the Church suffered enough?" concerned us. Since those early days of 2005, incredulous as it sounds, Judge Moore, as of 2020, became a member of the sexual abuse review board for the Archdiocese of New York, the same archdiocese over which he presides and judges the stories of victims of clergy sexual abuse.

I knew it was a long shot that my RICO claim would have succeeded because of the First Amendment rule of separation of Church and State, but I did know that the Church acted just like Mafia organizations, both financially and by eliminating its enemies. The Church is a racket, and it is as corrupt as any organization in the world. However, in 2005, the courts, law enforcement, and legislatures still thought the Church was a legitimate religious organization that led souls to God. I knew differently, as did those of us who were on the inside, but Judge Moore was not convinced and threw out the RICO claim in quick fashion, fining my attorney eight thousand dollars for filing a frivolous lawsuit. Once again, one institution (the court system) rallied around another (the Church) to attempt to silence free speech and the rights of individuals to seek justice. Judge Moore's catholicity and protection of it surfaced during practically every comment and ruling he made, thus denying me my right to claim that his Catholic Church was an organized criminal entity. Shortly before my claim was heard by Judge Moore, the Chief Justice of the Supreme Court, John Roberts, admonished federal judges across the country to recuse themselves more often when there was even an appearance of conflict of interest. If any judge had a claim more replete with conflict of interest and the necessity to recuse himself, it was Judge Moore.

Unfortunately, like Catholic popes, archbishops, and bishops who are heads of archdioceses and dioceses who tend to serve for life or until retirement (or transfer to another archdiocese or diocese by the life-serving Pope), United States federal judges are appointed for life and are tempted to rule with impunity. Judge Moore frequently turned beet-red when my attorney asked a perfectly appropriate question or commented about a legal matter. Needless to say, Judge Moore exhibited the same arrogance and elitism as many leaders, such as members of the Church hierarchy.

I announced my lawsuit before the New York and New Jersey media outlets on the third floor of a bar/restaurant in New York City. A former student's family owned the bar/restaurant and gave me carte blanche for its use. Most of the New York print and television media were present as were my supporters and my attorney.

My federal lawsuit was filed on December 13, 2005, and within only a few days, I received a telephone call from the office of Archbishop John J. Myers, ordering me to attend a meeting on December 20, 2005. It was Monsignor Louis Verducci, who held a number of positions within the Myers administration through the years; namely, secretary to the Archbishop, vicar general, chancellor, and vice chancellor, with whom we met. I told him I would not appear unless I had a canon lawyer with me. He said that would be fine, and I asked Msgr. Kenneth Lasch to accompany me to the meeting.

Msgr. Ken Lasch and I arrived at the chancery on Tuesday, December 20, 2005, and were immediately escorted to the office of Monsignor Verducci, who had his own alleged checkered history of improper sexual behavior with a female employee of the archdiocese. The next thing I knew, the parishioner who phoned me about the alleged sexual behavior went quiet. I wonder how the archdiocese resolved that claim?

The three of us sat at a small round table, and Verducci began the conversation. He began with, "Archbishop Myers has decided to suspend you from the priesthood, withdraw your faculties to function as a priest, and forbid that you present yourself as a priest publicly." He then handed me an official-looking document that had the word "Precept" in the title, indicating what Monsignor Louis Verducci had just told me. He also said, "I will have to take your identification card from you as well." The identification card for priests was introduced fairly recently by the bishops as the clergy sexual abuse crisis expanded. A priest was supposed to present that card to any other diocese he was to minister in to prove that he was a priest in good standing.

I opened my wallet and surrendered my identification card, declaring me a priest not in good standing.

Monsignor Verducci then outlined my salary and benefits plan. He said I would be paid as long as I was a priest in the archdiocese, and my health benefits would remain as well. I was thrilled to hear that since I thought Archbishop Myers would try to halt my salary and benefits and leave me destitute.

Msgr. Kenneth Lasch then also used canon law to describe my rights as a priest of the archdiocese. The meeting may have lasted fifteen minutes or so, and we were out of there. I felt relief like never before.

Four days later, which was the fourth Sunday of Advent and the day before Christmas, Archbishop Myers instructed that a letter be read in the two parishes where I currently served, explaining that I was a scandal to the archdiocese and the people of the archdiocese for filing a lawsuit against him, and that I had been suspended from the priesthood. Some parishioners phoned me to tell me about the letter and offer their support.

My attorney and I spoke at length about our next step, and we decided to appeal Judge Moore's decision to throw out my lawsuit. To file an appeal is a major ordeal. The paperwork had to be bound by a professional company, and it had to be done in triplicate since there are three appellate judges. We succeeded in filing the appeal and were called to New York Appellate Court in lower Manhattan.

The lead judge in the appeal was Sonia Sotomayor, who is currently a Supreme Court Justice. She was joined by another judge from the second circuit and a visiting judge from the ninth circuit. The first question she asked my attorney was, "Why didn't you bring the RICO claim to the appeal?" He answered, "Your Honor, Judge Moore fined me eight thousand dollars for what he determined to be a frivolous lawsuit. I couldn't risk the appeal court doing the same." We concluded that Judge Sotomayor might have considered the RICO claim, but it was too late. The three judges upheld Judge Moore's decision, which was a disappointment.

The next step was to file in the state superior court. That judge was a short, eccentric man who was difficult to comprehend at times. He eventually dismissed my claim based on the statute of limitations, so we were free to file in a neighboring state, but we believed the new court would dismiss it based on the statute of limitations as well.

All in all, my efforts with the judicial system started in 2005 and ended in 2010 with the final dismissal. The six years of court filings and proceedings may have seemed not to be successful, but my RICO filing in 2005 began a decades-long investigation of several members of the clergy. I was the first, as far as I know, to publicly discuss the sexual abuse by Cardinal Theodore McCarrick and his sleeping with seminarians. Some media outlets picked up on my lawsuit and ran with that news. Others were skeptical of many of my claims, but I knew and know they are true.

Robert M. Hoatson, Ph.D.

I felt disappointed in the judicial system, especially at the federal level, and it is my hope that Chief Justice Roberts reads this book to discover that at least one of his federal judges did not follow his instruction to recuse him or herself when there is even a hint of conflict, but at the same time, I feel good about the journey because it has opened up many doors for many others.

If I had filed my RICO case in 2017 or 2018, I think we may have had better success because the Church's reputation was being described as a Mafia organization by many Catholics and non-Catholics by that time. The judicial system, I felt, showed deference to the Catholic Church and all religions, and it had to stop. It was well worth the effort, since the defendants' lawyers had to spend hours and hours defending their clients and trying to convince court officers that the Church was on the up and up, which it wasn't, and has proven not to be.

By the time my lawsuits and appeals ended, Road to Recovery, Inc., was becoming a great success. We were collecting thousands of dollars in contributions yearly, and were able to help many victims with rent, clothing, food, and even legal fees. Since Father Ken and I were not taking salaries, we were able to focus financially on victims and their needs. That was to change dramatically for me in 2011.

One particular success story of our non-profit was that of Reginald Morris. Out of the blue, I received a lengthy letter from a southern prison. It was written in perfect English, as if a college English major had written it. He introduced himself as Reginald. He claimed to have been sexually abused by Father John Nickas at various places: in his car, at Father Nickas' rectory, and at a homeless shelter in Newark. He told me that years ago, his mother, who had her own serious problems, threw him out of their house for no apparent good reason. Reggie's neighbors, who were Catholics, had recommended he go see Father Nickas at St. Richard's Church, Newark, NJ, which he did.

CHAPTER FOURTEEN

THE MIRACLE STORY OF ASSISTING A VICTIM

Father Nickas took Reginald to the homeless shelter in a rough section of the city. Reginald was just a normal African-American young teenager from the inner-city who was intelligent, eloquent, and articulate. He was in a shelter with older men, including former prisoners and addicts. Reggie was sexually abused not only by Father Nickas in his car and at the rectory and church of St. Richard's but also by two brutes in the homeless shelter who had recently been freed from prison.

I developed a letter-writing campaign with Reginald, to and from the state prison in which he was held, and we finally decided that I should schedule a visit. We were trying to figure out how to get him released from prison despite his being there for holding up a Subway shop with a gun in a suburb of the metropolis in which he lived, which nearly scared the Asian owners, a husband and wife, to death. Since that was Reginald's second similar offense, (he held up a gas station about ten years earlier and served eight years for that crime), and the state in which he lived, Georgia, has a two-strikes-and-you're-in-prison-for-life penalty, he was facing that fate. However, the judge in the second case made a mistake and gave Reginald sixteen years rather than life in prison.

Reginald capitalized on the mistake made by the judge by filing a writ of *habeas corpus*. He hoped the appeal would be heard and the sentence commuted, but he also risked the judge realizing his mistake and re-assigning him to life in prison. Road to Recovery, Inc., hired a very experienced lawyer for Reginald, Bobby Joe Carter, for a few thousand dollars, and Reginald and his attorney began processing his appeal of the sentence. One day, I received a telephone call from Reginald's attorney, and he asked me, "Can you get down here tomorrow or the next day? Things are moving." I responded, "Yes, I am available." He then said, "Meet me at the headquarters of the County Prosecutor, and I will give you the lowdown when I see you."

I made plane reservations for the next day and flew immediately to Atlanta. I took the commuter monorail downtown and met Attorney Carter. He told me we were going to speak to the County District Attorney. I asked, "Who?" He said, "We have been called into the office of the County District Attorney because he wants to talk to you about Road to Recovery and your advocacy for Reginald Morris. It appears that Morris will be released to your custody. He was moved to the county jail, and there will be a hearing before the judge tomorrow morning in Superior Court. You'd better be ready to take Reginald back to New Jersey with you."

The meeting with the county district attorney went as well as any meeting I have ever attended. I compared the meeting where the District Attorney was respectful, complimentary, and thankful to the many meetings I had with Church leaders, who were just the opposite. I felt I was meeting with a genuine civil servant. He thanked me for my work with victims of sexual abuse, especially Reginald Morris, and he was aware of my communications with the state's commissioner of prisons, who was leading the country in changing prison policies and practices to reflect a more humane approach.

He asked me to confirm what I had been writing and communicating; namely, that Reginald Morris deserved to be released with time served and that he should be allowed to start his life over. It was crucial that Reggie had revealed his abuse to me and others because the district attorney felt that Reggie had pricked the abscess that had kept him imprisoned since he was a teenager. He then invited me to attend the hearing the next day in the courtroom of the judge.

When I left the office of the district attorney, I was overjoyed but overwhelmed at the same time. If Reginald was going to be released the next day, I had to make plans to drive him home. I rented a car and arranged for it to be dropped off at Newark Airport.

I could barely sleep that night, so I took a trip over to the county jail, which was on lockdown because the water system had broken down and the prisoners were rioting. I met a woman, a prison advocate, from the Southern Poverty Law Center who was advocating for more humane treatment of inmates, mostly from minority cities. My heart sank when I heard from the advocate that the Fulton County, Georgia, jail was one of the worst in the country. I thought I might have to stay several days before the water and calm were restored and Reginald would be released. Thankfully, the water system was repaired fairly quickly, but I wouldn't have wanted my worst enemy to spend an hour in the county jail. It was a several-story hellhole that reminded me of a third-world prison.

I finally fell asleep in the hotel, I guess, because I awoke suddenly from a sound sleep, thinking I had missed court that morning. I hurriedly headed for the county courthouse where I met Reginald's lawyer, Bobby Joe Carter. I was anxious to see if Reginald might be brought to the courthouse early, but I didn't see him until they called his case. He shuffled in with shackles on his hands and feet, but he gave me a smile as he approached the bench. The hearing was quick. The judge said a few things, and then he announced, "I understand that there is a Dr. Robert Hoatson in the gallery." I stood up and acknowledged that I was he. The judge asked me to step forward to give me some directions.

"Thank you, Dr. Hoatson, for your work on behalf of victims (he didn't reference sexual abuse victims so as not to embarrass Reginald, I am sure), and it is my understanding that you will be taking Mr. Morris back to New Jersey today." I replied, "Yes, Your Honor, I am ready to drive him to New Jersey." The judge then said, "Mr. Morris, you will be released from the county jail today to the custody of Dr. Hoatson. However, one of the mandates of your release is that you must never return to our state. Is that clear?" Reginald answered, "Yes, Your Honor, and thank you." His attorney thanked the judge as well. I nearly fell on the floor. My reaction to the miracle that took place for a clergy sexual abuse victim by a judge who did not know me except by reputation, released a prisoner to my custody, never to serve another day in prison was, "Pinch me." I looked at the attorney and we were both absolutely giddy with joy.

Reginald was taken from the courtroom and brought back to the county jail. I waited about four hours in the waiting room before I was called to enter the jail and be united with Reggie. He came to the front lobby with a bag of his belongings, and we left as fast as we could. Since it was already late in the day, I recommended that we grab a bite and get on the road so we would no longer be in that state. I didn't trust that if a state trooper saw that Reggie was in the car and was not supposed to enter the state anymore, we might not be believed.

We drove a few hours, making sure we left the state. I recommended we find a hotel in a neighboring state, and Reggie agreed. I reserved two rooms at a hotel just off the interstate, and I said good night to Reggie. It seems we both slept soundly that night, and the hotel we stayed in provided free breakfast the next morning. We were both somewhat anxious to get back on the road, but neither one of us knew exactly where we were headed.

Reggie's family still lived in the state we just had to leave— Georgia. He was still close to some family members, but had his mother not thrown him out of her Newark house when he was a young teenager, he probably would never have met Fr. John Nickas and the brutes in the homeless shelter. Reggie keeps in contact with some of his family, but he met a beautiful woman, an accomplished university librarian, and they began a relationship. The two of them drove to Newark from the South one weekend in order to demonstrate outside the church and rectory where Reggie was sexually abused. The pastor at the time, seeing us picketing outside his church as he drove from another parish he served, nearly turned a corner on two wheels, jumped out of his moving car, and blasted us verbally for being there. I thought he was going to become physical, so I reminded him that the First Amendment allows for free speech in the United States of America and that we were not on church property.

As part of my trip to Atlanta to witness the commuting of Reginald's sentence, I made it a point to visit the Asian couple who owned the Subway shop, and explain to them the history of Reginald's sexual abuse and the damage it caused, and hoped they would be forgiving. Actually, I only met with the husband because his wife has only been able to go back into the shop at various times because of her fear of being robbed. The husband was understanding and accepted my explanation. I asked him to give my best to his wife and guaranteed them both that Reginald Morris would never step foot in their state again.

Whenever the opportunity presents itself, I make it a point to visit the victims of crime, such as the Asian couple, because it is important for society to understand that sexual abuse of children affects every aspect of life, culturally, socially, spiritually, and psychologically.

It was very heartening for me to speak to the owner of the Subway Shop, a simple man just trying to make a living, but I cried internally for his wife who now, with her husband, must deal with aspects of post-traumatic stress disorder. The fact that the husband welcomed me and sat in a booth for a few minutes to listen to me, spoke loudly about the depth of integrity of that man and his wife. To them, every customer who walks into that shop now is a "Reggie Morris" and can't help but think every customer has a loaded gun hidden somewhere, ready to rob them. That will never abate completely. In addition, their extended family suffers the same trauma as well because they worry twenty-four hours a day and seven days a week about their relatives and their customers.

Reggie and I had many hours to talk on the way back to New Jersey. Reggie had no family there, and I didn't exactly have a plan for his recovery, since what happened while I was there was a miracle. It made no sense logically, so I believe God was working overtime on that case. I told Reggie that Road to Recovery, Inc. could put him up in a motel near Newark Airport for a week or so, but I needed him to think carefully about what we might do long term. I dropped him off at a convenient hotel next door to Newark Airport, and returned the car at the airport. I picked up my car at the long-term parking lot and headed home to Rockaway Beach.

The next day, I met Reggie so we could begin to get his life back to normalcy. We visited a clothing store and bought him some basic clothing and shoes. We ate breakfast together and started to strategize. Reginald said he had no benefits, and it would be difficult to find a two-time felon a decent job. I told him we had a week to get things together before his hotel stay ran out, and in a last-ditch effort, I asked him if he had ever been in the military. He said, "Yes, I served in the active-duty army." I almost ran off the road when I heard that good news, and I headed directly to East Orange, New Jersey, where there is an enormous veterans' hospital and facility.

We entered the veterans' home, and we were immediately greeted by an employee who asked us how he could help us. We told him what we needed, and we headed to the waiting room to register for veterans' benefits. Reggie was called to a cubicle, where an African-American woman asked how she could help him. I could not accompany him to the cramped cubicle. He told the woman he was a veteran and served in active duty. She then looked up Reggie's records, and they had a fairly lengthy conversation that was interrupted with laughter and banter. It looked good to me.

The registration lady handed Reggie a set of papers, and my heart began to beat loudly. Reggie was happy, too. He told me another miracle story. He said the woman, after looking up his records, indicated to him that he had served a total of 23 months in active duty and that he needed to serve 24 months of active duty to receive full benefits. "I was devastated," Reginald told me, "and I thought it was all over." The woman then said to Reginald with a wink and a nod, "Don't worry, Reginald Morris, my computer now indicates that you served 24 months in active duty, and you now have full benefits." When Reginald told me that story, I got the attention of the woman and mouthed, "Thank you." I had a tear in my eye, as did Reggie.

Since Reginald now had full benefits through the Veterans' Administration, he received a full medical and psychiatric workup. He was assigned to live at the veterans' home in west-central New Jersey, and he immediately was treated for post-traumatic stress disorder and other medical issues. He was fed, clothed, and taken care of by the United States of America. We also began to strategize as to how to hold Father John Nickas accountable.

During Reggie's time at the veterans' hospital, his abuser, Father John Nickas, died. Nickas was living in a priests' retirement home in New Jersey, and was granted a full priest's funeral at a church next door to the retirement home. The Archdiocese had been informed of Reggie's allegation against Father Nickas, and that he intended to seek justice. Reggie's counselor recommended that he attend Father Nickas' funeral as a way of getting some closure to his serious sexual abuse.

Reggie asked me to accompany him to the funeral, and he and I sat in the last pew of the church in case the funeral created too much anxiety for him. As soon as we walked into the church and sat down, the infamous Joseph Devine of the archdiocese asked two local detectives to stand behind us in the church. I guess he thought we might interrupt the funeral. We stayed until the homily, which was a whitewash of the life of Father John Nickas. Reggie could not listen to any more accolades for the priest who abused him, so we went outside and stood on the sidewalk in front of the church. The two detectives followed us. We got into a great discussion with the detectives, who understood what happened to Reggie. One of the detectives told us that he was married by a priest from the same parish and that priest, the former pastor, was removed from the priesthood for sexually abusing children. Two of us uttered in unison, "You can't make it up."

Reggie and I waited for the procession to leave the church with the casket, and Reginald Morris made his peace quietly with Father John Nickas. We then left without being greeted by the archbishop or any other clerics who knew about the allegations against the deceased John Nickas. It gave Reggie a startling education about how the Catholic Church handles clergy sexual abuse allegations. We said goodbye to the detectives with whom we had become friendly and left.

CHAPTER FIFTEEN

ROAD TO RECOVERY'S HUMBLE BEGINNINGS

During the early 2000s, I started to become more involved with other victim/survivors and advocates. Msgr. Kenneth Lasch, pastor of St. Joseph's Parish, Mendham, NJ, opened a hall in the parish for sexual abuse victims to have weekly support meetings. In 2003, I began attending those meetings, and they were enormously helpful. In the early days, we had about thirty attendees, but once settlements were reached with many victims, they received a well-deserved degree of closure and worked on putting their entire nightmare of clergy sexual abuse behind them.

Eventually, the new pastor of the parish, Father Wallace, did not welcome us and withdrew the invitation to continue to meet there. Fortunately, the local Methodist church welcomed us. We held meetings there for several years. After that, the meeting was moved to a victim's home in the urban area, which was not ideal, but sufficed. Now we meet in a conference room of a local business nearby.

The western New Jersey meetings at St. Joseph's were particularly powerful and poignant because of the leadership and concern of Lou and Pat Serrano, the parents of Mark Serrano, a student at a major Catholic university. During one of his college breaks, he revealed to his parents that he had been abused. Lou and Pat immediately went into overdrive regarding justice for their son and other boys who were abused. They collaborated with Msgr. Kenneth Lasch, the successor to Father James Hanley, and began helping Mark and many others recover from horrific sexual abuse. Pat Serrano became a victims' contact person for an international advocacy agency, and she and I worked together to make sure that no victim who contacted either of us would be denied assistance.

One day, I received a call from a man who said that Pat Serrano had recommended he call me. He was from Montclair, New Jersey, the next town over from where I live, so I told him I could meet him right away. We decided to meet under the trees at a Montclair park, an idyllic setting with a lake. I knew the park well since my father's brother's family, Uncle Jim and Aunt Alice and their four children, lived a few blocks from there, and as kids, we used to ice skate there when we visited my relatives' house.

I met the gentleman who called. He introduced himself as Kevin Waldrip. He drove a simple car, which was crowded with clothing, blankets, and lots of other things. It looked like he had been living in the car. We talked for a few minutes on a park bench, but it became breezy and cold, so we went into my car. Kevin told me that was he a native of Newark, New Jersey, and was, indeed, living in his car. He parked his car each night in a Montclair lot and slept there. He said he had been doing that for a few years. He told me he was sexually abused by Father Richard Galdon at Our Lady of Good Counsel Parish, the same parish that I had been stationed at as Director of Schools from 2001–2003. Richard Galdon was a famous name, since he was the first Newark archdiocesan priest to be arrested and put in prison for many years. He was a serial pedophile of Good Counsel students, altar servers, and boy scouts during his many years at Our Lady of Good Counsel.

Before his arrest and incarceration, however, he spent many months at the Servants of the Paraclete Rehabilitation Center in Jemez Springs, New Mexico. Bishops sent many pedophiles and alcoholics to that church-run facility for decades. The founder of the Servants of the Paraclete and the rehabilitation center, Father Gerald Fitzgerald, once recommended to the bishops that they purchase a deserted island in the Caribbean and place the pedophile priests there because they were incapable of being rehabilitated and posed an ongoing danger to children, teenagers, and vulnerable adults. Richard Galdon was one such incorrigible pedophile.

Kevin Waldrip told me that he was sexually abused once by Father Richard Galdon, on his 14th birthday—February 1, 1965. Galdon caught him smoking, and Kevin was ordered into Galdon's office in the rectory, where Galdon had his way with him. It changed Kevin's life forever. Kevin tried to get through his freshman year at nearby Essex Catholic High School, but he was not able to focus or concentrate. His grades were too low for him to continue, so he ended up at St. James High School in the Ironbound section of Newark, but he dropped out shortly thereafter. He spent his teenage years and the rest of his life trying to survive.

I asked Kevin if he wanted me to get him a hotel room using Road to Recovery funds, but he declined. Instead, he asked me to help him deal with the abuse, so I invited him to the support meetings at St. Joseph's, and he became a regular attendee. He became strong enough to look into benefits through the government. Road to Recovery helped him with some funds for food and an attorney, and he eventually was granted permanent disability. He lived in his own apartment in Old Bridge, New Jersey, and had a Volkswagen that he purchased with funds from his disability settlement until his death in 2021.

Kevin could have easily "retired" and lived less stressfully after receiving medical and living benefits, but he became one of the most active advocates in the country. He attended hundreds of press conferences, demonstrations, protests, and other events that supported thousands of other victims. Kevin did not let his damage and "issues" stop him from going public about his own case, which he boldly did in the *Newark Star Ledger*, and standing with other victims when they announced their own abuse. Unfortunately, as Kevin got older, his health did not allow him to do as much as he was used to doing, but he attended our support meetings and continued to follow the "survivor movement" with great interest. He and I would laugh about the several times we were nearly arrested when we challenged law enforcement officers (usually called by Catholic Church officials to silence us) about our First Amendment rights of free speech and assembly.

After Kevin's story appeared in the *Newark Star Ledger*, a classmate and neighbor of his from Our Lady of Good Counsel Parish in Newark contacted Kevin. Jerome Zakowski's family lived in the North Ward for decades, and when Jerome saw the story of Kevin in the newspaper, his heart went out to him. He became a good friend and advocate for Kevin. Jerome was thankful Father Richard Galdon never sexually abused him, despite the fact that Jerome was a very active student and parishioner. Jerome often worked with Father Galdon to run off papers on the old mimeograph machines in the basement of the elementary school building, and was also an altar server. Galdon did, however, take Jerome to the Galdon family summer home on Greenwood Lake, New York, and the family home in Hudson County. In fact, the Galdons had a working train set in the Hudson County home, which was a "grooming" technique for Father Richard.

Unfortunately, Jerome did not go un-abused through his life. The superintendent of his apartment building where his family lived, sexually abused him. Jerome continues to be a regular at support meetings and is there whenever we need help with victims. Ironically, Jerome was one year ahead of me at Essex Catholic High School (1969), was in the honors program, and became captain of the vocations club. I was a member of that club and eventually became a Christian Brother. Jerome had better sense and avoided religious life and the priesthood, although he remains a practicing Catholic. His beautiful young wife died of cancer many years ago, and he has been leading a bereavement group in his parish for many years. Jerome has two daughters, one who is a highly qualified nurse and the other a member of national law enforcement.

Tragically, Jerome died suddenly as this book was being published.

Shortly after Msgr. Kenneth Lasch and I founded Road to Recovery, Inc., I began thinking more and more about clergy sexual abuse, sexual abuse in general, and people who possibly showed signs of having been sexually abused. I knew about my own post-traumatic stress disorder, and I noticed others with similar symptoms as myself.

Support meetings for me were a great help because I knew I wasn't alone. One of the people I couldn't get off my mind was my first cousin, Jimmy Craig Hoatson. Many years before, I had heard a story about my Uncle Jim (Jimmy's father and my father's older brother) confronting a Christian Brother and telling him to stay away from his son. At the time, I didn't think anything of it, but the revelations of my own abuse by Christian Brothers brought that memory back in pretty vivid detail. I wondered how I could find out more. By this time, my family was familiar with my advocacy on behalf of victims, and my demonstrations in front of churches and protests elsewhere began to be covered extensively by radio, television, and print media.

In Memory Of

JAMES CRAIG HOATSON
CLASS OF 1967
*Your Family, Friends and Classmates
Will Never Forget You*

Robert M. Hoatson, Ph.D.

CHAPTER SIXTEEN

JIMMY CRAIG HOATSON, MY FIRST COUSIN

I decided to phone my cousin, Linda, Jimmy Craig Hoatson's sister, who is my age. Linda attended East Orange Catholic High School for Girls for nearly three years before the family moved to South New Jersey. We both graduated high school in 1970. It took me days to finally pick up the phone and call. Linda is a blonde-haired, blue-eyed, pretty young woman of Scottish-Polish heritage who is a realtor. She married a very successful painting contractor. Nervously, I said to Linda, "I am calling to ask you a very personal question that has been bothering me for a while." Then I just came out with it: "Was Jimmy ever sexually abused at Essex Catholic High School for Boys?" The reason I couldn't call Jimmy himself was that he had killed himself in 1978 with a shotgun, leaving his father, mother, sisters, brother, wife, two sons, and a large extended family.

Linda was ready to talk, thank goodness. She responded, "Yes, Jimmy was sexually abused by his science teacher, Brother Jerome Heustis." I gasped, nearly cried, but held it together somehow. "Linda, I am so sorry. I sensed that something happened to Jimmy since I began to acknowledge my own sexual abuse in the Christian Brothers." She empathized with my abuse, and we continued talking. I asked her if she could give me any details about Jimmy and Brother Jerome Heustis, who, by the way, was a proficient musician, moderator of the school choir, and my sophomore religion teacher. Jimmy and I were in the choir together, but Jimmy's participation in the choir made no sense to me—ever. Jimmy was a jock, and choir would have been the last activity with which I would have associated him. After speaking to Linda, however, it made sense based on my personal and professional analysis of sexual abuse, that Jimmy was "forced" to join the choir and was "forced" to keep that secret. When both of our fathers showed up for the Christmas concert when I was a freshman and Jimmy was a junior, it was puzzling to me.

How did Brother Jerome Heustis get access to Jimmy? He first saw him in science class and then began to "groom" him. He wrote him love notes and gave him gifts. One of the gifts he gave him, according to Linda, was the 45 RPM record "Cherish" by The Association, a popular singing group at the time from California. Their music was described by some as sunshine pop. Linda then reminded me of the lyrics: "Cherish is the word I use to describe / All the feeling that I have hiding here for you inside / You don't know how many times I wished that I had told you / You don't know how many times I've wished that I could hold you / You don't know how many times I've wished that I could mold you into someone / Who could cherish me as much as I cherish you."

"Oh my God," I said to Linda, "I am so sorry for you and your family." I then asked Linda if Heustis was the Christian Brother who was told by her father to leave his son alone. Linda was not positive of that, but there was another Christian Brother who pursued Jimmy, too: Brother John Adrian Reidy, who rode a motorcycle and used to show up at the Hoatson home in Upper Montclair. Linda could not verify that but thought she remembered Brother John Adrian Reidy being at the house. Finally, Linda said to me, "Bob, don't let this out to anyone, please. My mother is still alive, and she just couldn't bear this being made public." I promised her that our conversation was confidential. Her mother, my Aunt Alice, has died since.

When I hung up the phone, I didn't know whether to throw something across the room or fall on the floor crying. Jimmy was killed because of sexual abuse by a religious brother. His funeral at St. Cassian's Church in Upper Montclair, New Jersey, was a total fog, and most of the family can't remember the day at all. I did the prayers at the graveside but don't remember much about it. The shock was so palpable that I cannot tell you where the repast[4] took place. The whole family was shocked that such a handsome, athletic man of 29 years would kill himself, because it appeared he had the world at his fingertips. He spent summers at the Jersey Shore surfing and swimming, and if he were in California, he would have been called a surfer dude.

Linda, at the time, had told me I couldn't make Jimmy's story public, but she did say I could work behind the scenes to report Brother Jerome Heustis. Within days of our conversation, I phoned Brother Joseph Gattone, provincial of the Western American Province of the Christian Brothers. After Brother Jerome Heustis was stationed at Essex Catholic High School in Newark, New Jersey, the Christian Brothers split into different provinces, and since Heustis was a native of the west coast, he decided to go west and teach in places like California and Illinois. I reported Jimmy's story to Brother Joseph Gattone, and he took down the details. Two weeks after the report was submitted, Brother Jerome Heustis died of a massive heart attack. I informed Linda about Brother Jerome Heustis' death, and she opined, and I agreed, that the news of the abuse must have caused his heart to fail. As far as Brother John Adrian Reidy is concerned, he died a few years ago, but several years ago when I was visiting Bishop Carney High School in Rochester, New York, where he was stationed for many years, he asked me out of the blue, "How is your cousin Jimmy doing?" I said to him, "Jimmy killed himself." I left it at that.

Since the New Jersey Child Victims Act (CVA) had passed, I asked Linda if the family wanted to file a claim on Jimmy's behalf. Linda said, "No, my mother would never be able to handle it."

Her mother, my Aunt Alice and Jimmy's mother, lived until 93 and had been one of my most vocal supporters. She used social media, like Facebook, to thank me for all that Road to Recovery,

---

4 Gathering after a funeral service

Inc. had done to help victims, and I had a sense Aunt Alice realized I was working for justice for her son, too.

Now that Aunt Alice was deceased, I asked Linda if she and her family changed their minds about filing a claim. "If you think it would help his two sons, then let's do it," Linda said. However, according to the Child Victims Act, it was too late to apply for a claim.

The new law in New Jersey allowed all those who were sexually abused as children or adults two years to come forward to hold their abusers accountable in courts of law. In other words, from 2019–2021, there was no statutory limit for those who were sexually abused at any time in their lives in the state of New Jersey. Once the two-year "window" closed in 2021, certain statutory limitations took over again. It took advocates and their supporters—most importantly, Senator Joseph Vitale and SNAP (Survivors Network of Those Abused by Priests') New Jersey leader, Mark Crawford, and activists like Fred Marigliano, who, at 69 years of age, walked from the southern tip of New Jersey to its northern border, to raise awareness of child sexual abuse—almost twenty years to change the laws in the state of New Jersey. Fortunately, both houses of the state legislature were controlled by the Democrats, and the governor, Phil Murphy, is a Democrat, so it was much easier for us to get the bill passed. In addition, many of the legislators, even Democrats who were "on the fence" about changing the law, were convinced once the sexual abuse by Archbishop McCarrick, former Archbishop of Newark, who ordained me to the priesthood in 1997, became public.

2019 was a banner year for victim/survivors, advocates, supporters, and the general public. Both New Jersey and New York passed laws referred to as "Child Victims Acts." In New York, the law only applied to those who were sexually abused as children when they were under the age of 18, and their "window" was to last only one year. It was scheduled to close in August, 2020, but because of the Covid-19 pandemic, the original sponsors of the New York bill, Senator Brad Hoylman and Assemblywoman Linda Rosenthal, asked the legislature to extend the window another year.

The legislature passed a year-long extension, and then-Governor Andrew Cuomo signed the bill, extending the window to August, 2021.

The New York bill, like the one in New Jersey, was the culmination of twenty years of lobbying a Republican Senate and Democratic Assembly. The Assembly passed the bill after many years through the heroic work of Assemblywoman Marge Markey, but the Republican Senate refused to allow the bill to be voted on. Once the Senate turned Democratic in 2019, we were fairly certain the legislature would vote in our favor, and then-Governor Andrew Cuomo promised on several occasions that if a Child Victims Act bill ended up on his desk, he would sign it immediately.

On the day that the New York Senate was to finally pass the bill, then-Governor Cuomo invited approximately fifteen of us victims and advocates to his private chambers to celebrate the passage of the bill and thank us for our perseverance. He then invited us to join him at a press conference in the governor's media center, where he lauded the passage of the bill and the courage all of us exhibited in lobbying year after year for the bill's passage. Former Governor Cuomo's office sent each of us several photos of the morning we spent with him, and I have those photos framed on the walls of my apartment. I was so happy to have been involved in the passage of both states' bills. Since then, California passed a Child Victims Act with a three-year window. The states are gradually changing their laws to favor victims rather than predators. When I began lobbying and advocating for both bills, I dedicated my work to my cousin Jimmy Craig Hoatson and asked for his intervention from heaven.

Robert M. Hoatson, Ph.D.

PART II

Robert M. Hoatson, Ph.D.

CHAPTER SEVENTEEN

AN INSIDER'S EXPERIENCE

You might recall from an earlier chapter that I took a detour in my talk with Msgr. Kenneth Lasch in 2002 in order to describe the sexual abuse by Brother Martin Francis Connelly. My meeting with Father Ken focused primarily on the sexual abuse I endured from the ages of approximately thirteen until thirty, when Brother Frank, for the last time, abused me in my bedroom at Catholic Memorial High School in 1982. However, our conversation went back and forth between Father Ken's experience of decades of priesthood and my five years of priesthood. I shared with him five years of abuse that emanated from the culture of clericalism and the corruption and dysfunction of the hierarchy. This section goes in depth of my experience inside the hierarchy of the Catholic Church and what I witnessed and endured.

Of course, Fr. Ken was interested in the fact that I was already in my third assignment as a priest in just a few years, so I took some time to intersperse what happened to me during those years. I told Father Ken, "I was propositioned in the seminary just before I was ordained a deacon." I was 42 years old; he was 27. Seminarian Mario Ventura had first approached me when I attended my first "Pub Night" in the seminary community room. It was towards the end of the evening where pizza, beer, and soda had been purchased by the seminary for the seminarians. I was introducing myself to the other seminarians for the first time, and a short, very good-looking young man approached the table at which I was sitting and introduced himself. He then said to me that he had heard that I had been a golf professional in my earlier life.

I told him, "Yes, I was the assistant golf professional at Fairmount Country Club in Chatham Township, New Jersey, for approximately a year." He then asked me, "Do you give lessons?" I told him I would be glad to teach him the basics of golf but that I didn't know our seminary schedule, and I asked him if we would have time to engage in golf lessons. He mentioned that we were free on Sunday afternoons, for the most part, so I said Sunday afternoons were a good time to get on a public golf course. I told him, "We can probably start when the weather changes." It was January when we first spoke.

"Pub Night" was an interesting tradition in the seminary. I came to find out that for many, it was a pick-up joint for men like Mario Ventura. He may have wanted to learn how to play golf, but what he really wanted was me. One afternoon, after almost a year of teaching him to play golf and becoming quite friendly, we had gone to a local public course on a Sunday afternoon and played eighteen holes. Needless to say, both of us needed a shower. I asked Mario if he wanted to go to the cafeteria after getting cleaned up to get something to eat. He said, "Sure, knock on my door when you get showered and dressed." I said, "Okay."

I finished showering and dressing and headed down the hall to Mario's room. I knocked and heard him yell, "Come on in, I am still showering." I entered his sitting room and sat down on his couch. His television was on at the time, so I changed the station to the PGA tournament. I don't remember which golf tournament was on, but it didn't matter, because a PGA tournament on Sunday, the final day, is usually interesting and competitive.

Finally, Mario came out of the shower and went into his bedroom. Mario was one of the few seminarians who occupied two rooms because there weren't enough seminarians to fill all the rooms. The typical seminary suite was a small combination of two bedrooms, with a bathroom in the middle that was shared by two seminarians. Mario did not have a "suite mate," so he used two bedrooms and the bathroom for himself.

He then came through the bathroom hallway from the bedroom and entered the sitting room. He was wearing boxer shorts and had a towel in his arm. He went over near the window of the room, turned to me, and said, "Bob, if you want to be my friend, you'll have to be my bitch." I did a double take and said, "What?" He then responded, "Oh, what are you gonna say now, that I'm gay?" I responded, "Well, Mario, as far as I know, that is a statement that one gay man says to another. I am not a gay man, Mario."

We did go to the cafeteria for something to eat, but I was convinced that it was time to distance myself from Mario. Apparently, he had made a comment to another seminarian a few months before this incident that "This new guy Bob is a good-looking guy, and he has perfect hair," but I didn't find that out until after we were ordained priests. Having been told that, "Pub Night" back in January now made sense. Mario wasn't really interested in learning how to play golf; he wanted the good-looking guy with the perfect hair. That jibed with my sense of the seminary in general.

It was a pick-up joint, and I think I was one of the few seminarians who was not acting out sexually in some way, either with priest professors, fellow seminarians, university students, or others. There was a rumor that one of our seminary staff members had the AIDS virus from surfing a local park for male partners. He told one of my classmates not to identify him as a priest when he had seen him at the Jersey Shore.

Sex was the operative climate throughout the seminary. I will never forget the first time I ate in the seminary dining room in between classes. The seminary faculty had to walk through the seminarians' dining room to get to their private dining room. I was astonished when I heard an obviously gay seminarian tell those at our table, "There goes Kitty, there goes Mary, and there goes Sally." He was referring to male members of the seminary faculty. "Two of the three professors are in a relationship, you know, and have a house at the Jersey Shore together."

I did not report Mario Ventura at the time. I did not want to report the incident to the rector of the seminary at the time, in particular. I was only a few weeks away from being ordained a deacon, so I thought I would be thrown out of the seminary if I reported Mario Ventura's proposition. I would have called for Mario to be removed, but as a relatively new person in the seminary, I was almost sure that I would have been the one to be asked to leave. Mario had "connections" among the seminary faculty, especially with Father Arthur Serratelli, who became Bishop Arthur Serratelli, and it was the faculty of the seminary who most often determined the fate of men preparing for the priesthood. I wish I had had more courage at the time. The time would come for reporting him, though.

Since I was older and had lots of experience in ministry and a Ph.D. already, I was assigned to a parish after ordination to the diaconate. Sadly, the associate pastor of Saint Margaret of Cortona Parish, Father Vincent, died during a day off while he was visiting the Empire State Building. The parish was devastated because he was a beloved priest. The pastor was not as beloved as the associate pastor, and was now at the parish by himself after Father Vincent died. Archbishop McCarrick assigned me as a deacon to Saint Margaret of Cortona in a suburban city in June, 1996, in order to provide diaconate help to the parish and the pastor. When I showed up with my belongings, the pastor was in the sacristy either preparing for Mass or just finishing. I walked into the sacristy and introduced myself, "Hi, Father, I am Deacon Bob, the new deacon." The pastor replied, "I don't need you; I need a priest." I thought to myself, *Another nut I have to deal with.*

Father Joseph Shannon had been a military man, an Air Force chaplain. He had risen through the ranks and reached an impressive level. He acted very much like the military man he was. Although I tend to like no-nonsense people in general, this pastor was too much. Thankfully, he treated clerics with respect, so I was off the hook. As far as lay people were concerned, he fluctuated between being a dictator and a pastor. It was hard to tell which personality was going to come through from day to day.

I got right to work, visiting parishioners in the hospital, counting the Saturday collection, directing the Pre-Cana Program, reading the Gospel at liturgies, and preaching. The parishioners came to enjoy my homilies because I tended to apply the gospel message to real life. I also stood in the back of the church after each Mass and greeted the parishioners. There were two Sisters of Saint Joseph on the parish staff when I arrived, and one of them particularly got under the pastor's skin. She had been there a long time and directed many of the parish activities while she was there. She was very popular with many parishioners, so the pastor tolerated her for a little while longer. She eventually left, and the other sister remained for a very long time as Director of Religious Education.

Father Shannon and I generally got along, and I knew it would only be for a year since I would be ordained a priest in May, 1997. As my attachment to the parish and parishioners grew, however, I was hoping that Archbishop McCarrick would see fit to let me remain in the parish as a priest. One of the trustees of the parish wrote to Archbishop McCarrick, asking him to assign me to the parish after ordination, as did some other parishioners. Pastorally, they saw me as a good "foil" to the gruffer and snarlier Father Joseph Shannon. For example, Father Joseph Shannon made no plans liturgically for Holy Week. As we got closer to Palm Sunday, I wondered how we were going to coordinate the ministers, choir, and celebrants to have meaningful Masses on Palm Sunday. Thank God someone ordered palms for the parishioners because there would have been hell to pay had there been no palms.

Another priest had been assigned to our parish a few months earlier, and he and I got together to discuss how the parish was going to celebrate Holy Week appropriately. We patched together three liturgies for Holy Thursday, Good Friday, and Easter Sunday, and most of the parishioners didn't know the difference. They followed the missalettes that were provided, but as far as "extras," there were none. I hoped that I could experience a proper Holy Week once I became a priest.

CHAPTER EIGHTEEN

MY ORDINATION

In May, 1997, I was ordained a priest in one of the most beautiful cathedrals in the country, if not the world. There were approximately twenty of us who became priests that day, the largest class in the United States that year. It was very important for Archbishop McCarrick's ego that he have the largest ordination class in the country because the pope was very impressed by large ordination classes. McCarrick was always hobnobbing with the rich and famous, including titans of Hollywood and Wall Street, and he had all of them hoodwinked. He was a prolific fund-raiser, which endeared him to the pope and the Vatican. It was rumored that when the pope visited the United States in 1995, he returned to Rome with a stash of cash from various sources. Where did the money come from? Who knows, but you can be sure that it was from a host of sources.

A couple of weeks after ordination, my ordination class was called to the residence of the archbishop to receive our first priestly assignments. When Archbishop McCarrick came to me, he said, "Bobby, I am sending you to a good guy, Colman Finneran, at St. Luke's in Hudson County." Archbishop McCarrick had a habit of calling younger men by their "childish nicknames," such as Bobby, Billy, Artie, and Donnie. I thanked the archbishop and began to get excited about starting my ministry as a priest. I knew almost nothing about Hudson County, though I had attended a prior diaconate ordination at St. Veronica Parish, the northernmost parish in the city.

St. Luke's is part of the Hudson County peninsula, surrounded on the west by Newark Bay, on the south by the Kill Van Kull, on the east by New York Bay (near the Statue of Liberty), and on the north by Jersey City. A bridge connects Hudson County and New York City, and St. Luke's was accessible from that bridge and some highways.

I was 45 years old when I was ordained a priest. When I had met with Archbishop McCarrick in 1994 when I was considering becoming a priest, he said to me, "Oh, Bobby, you are only 42, and you're in good shape. I need strong horses for the long haul."

I arrived at St. Luke's Parish in early June, 1997, and moved into the rooms occupied by Father Herbert Knox, who was leaving to become the secretary to Archbishop McCarrick. He was a tall priest and a musician. He was eager to become a heavy-hitter in the church. After I moved in, I stripped and shellacked the beautiful wooden floors in both my sitting room and bedroom. When Father Herb found out that I closed my doors at night for privacy, he admonished me one day by saying, "I never closed those doors once when I lived there." I said, "Good for you," but ignored his ignorant comment because he was unaware of my history of sexual abuse in religious houses.

Some of the clergy of the archdiocese called the Hudson County peninsula "The Archdiocese of Hudson County" because of its remoteness, difficulty in traveling to, and various industries like oil refineries, ports, and largely undeveloped land that was thought to be toxic. There were numerous parishes in the peninsula, including a cathedral-sized church called St. Peter's, which was located in the center of the peninsula. Ethnic parishes dotted the city, too, with Lithuanian, Polish, Irish, and Italian parishes often only a few blocks apart. St. Luke's was the more typical Catholic parish because it was situated at the south end of the peninsula and boasted mostly Irish parishioners.

Hudson County in 1997 was middle America par-excellence. American flags hung from thousands of homes, which were only a few feet apart, and July 4th and the St. Patrick's Day parades were major social and civic events throughout the county. The pastor of St. Luke's, Colman Finneran, was a kind, jolly man who was well loved by parishioners and many other Hudson County residents, especially firefighters. After Archbishop McCarrick assigned me to St. Luke's, I took a ride to Hudson County to get an idea of what the church, rectory, and school looked like. As I approached the parish, I noticed the church steeple and deduced that the house across the street was the rectory. I wasn't sure because there was an antique fire engine sitting in the driveway behind the house.

I drove past that house and continued on toward the church. It was on a busy corner with a traffic light, and the parish school was diagonally across the street. St. Luke's was a beautiful edifice, the kind of "real" church I liked. It wasn't "modern" like those in the round or those that looked like airline hangars. It was a fairly large church, and the landscaping around the church made it attractive. I then continued down the block to the dead end, which I assumed was the end of the peninsula, just four blocks away. As I approached what looked like a river, I became frightened to death.

An enormous tanker was going up the county waterway, but because of the slight rise in the street I was traveling on at that point, the tanker, in an optical illusion, actually appeared to be on land near me. I slowed to a crawl until the tanker passed. I then proceeded to drive to the end of the street and parked. I got out and took a walk to the waterway. It was a narrow waterway, making it easy to get a good look at a tugboat company based on the opposite side of the waterway. I realized then that the section in which St. Luke's was located was a major thoroughfare for products and goods to the New York area. I liked what I saw, and I especially liked that I was so close to New York City and my favorite things—Broadway shows.

However, as I became acclimated to St. Luke's Parish, I discovered that I might be confronting some significant dysfunctions and practices. First of all, one of the first conversations I had with the pastor was about saying Mass. Father Colman Finneran said to me, "Bob, if you don't want to show up for Masses, don't worry about it." I then asked, "Colman, if I don't show up for Masses, who will say them?" He then said, "Don't worry, someone will cover them." I thought to myself, "What the hell was I ordained for?" Needless to say, I did not miss Masses when I was assigned them.

The next thing Father Colman told me was, "Bob, we each have two full days off. I am off Tuesday and Wednesday; you can take Thursday and Friday." While most priests might jump at having two days off, I reminded myself that archdiocesan policy allowed each priest a day and a half off. Normally, a priest would say the earliest morning Mass on the day he was leaving for his day off and then be back the next evening. I said, "Okay, Colman. I am not used to that because I took a day and a half when I was a deacon." No one checked up on Father Colman, so there was never a change in the practice.

Shortly after, Father Philip Fabiano, my former pastor from Sacred Heart Parish in Yonkers, New York, whose health forced him to receive a liver transplant in 1995, moved into St. Luke's rectory. I had asked Father Finneran if he could live with us for a while and help out in the parish as he continued to recover from his transplant. He had been transferred from Sacred Heart Parish in 1993, despite asking for another year. I spent five of my most enjoyable years at that parish as an educational administrator. Had he been given another year of pastorate, I would have stayed until he finished his seventh year, but the leadership of his religious order would not allow it, and they assigned a different priest as pastor, and that priest and I did not see eye-to-eye. Father Philip Fabiano was a transformational leader.

I feel more comfortable working with leaders who are creative and risk-taking. The new pastor was a status-quo type of leader.

My priest friend and I got busy working on the rectory at St. Luke's. I painted practically the entire first and second floor staircases, which badly needed sprucing up, and I also began working on the church, first by washing the altar server outfits and cleaning the sacristy and altar server areas. The church was not cleaned on a regular basis. The only custodian hired in the parish was the school custodian, and he didn't clean the church. Some women parishioners purportedly straightened out the church after weekend services, but there was never a full cleaning of the church, including vacuuming. The choir loft was in shambles, and I feared at times that it would detach from the church and cave into the nave. Father Colman didn't seem to see the need for major renovations at that time.

To say that Father Colman Finneran was a laid-back pastor would be an understatement. His laid-back style made him very pastorally sensitive, and he would get in his car and respond to anyone who called for a priest. That style enabled me, as a rookie priest, to preside at the Easter Vigil that year in his place and not only administer baptism, but confirmation as well. We were supposed to get permission from the regional bishop in order to confirm, but that didn't bother Father Colman. When I asked him if he received permission for me to perform confirmations, he laughed and said, "Of course." Colman's ego never got in the way at any time, and he did not lord it over priests and parishioners, but other aspects of his leadership were concerning to me.

The parish was busy. We had quite a few funerals annually, and a few weddings, but the church was not an ideal place for weddings because it was not in good shape. Such a beautiful church deserved better care. The rectory was not much better. When I arrived, the rectory was a mess in many ways. The pastor allowed members of Alcoholics Anonymous to meet in the basement and smoke indoors. I am highly allergic to cigarette smoke, so I went to Father Colman and asked him to ban smoking in the rectory entirely. He was very amenable and told AA that smoking had to be done outside the rectory. However, the remnants of tar and nicotine in the basement were caked on the walls and floor and ceiling. So, I put my mask on and thoroughly cleaned the basement. It took more than a week to return the basement to some semblance of cleanliness.

The basement of the rectory also housed the food pantry, which was a terrific ministry to the hungry of Hudson County. Unfortunately, there was no procedure for distributing the food, so anyone at any time could ring the rectory bell and ask for a food package. It created some resentment among the parish staff and priests since the staff would have to leave their work stations, often fill up bags with food, and then carry them up the stairs to the front door. They would call the priests if we were around, but we were often involved with other aspects of ministry. The pastor didn't think we needed a schedule to give out food, like other parishes had. Besides, the pastor became friends with several of the homeless, and he stopped everything to help them.

Father Colman Finneran's laid-back and somewhat cavalier style of leadership was problematic at times. He was a fire buff, which explained the antique fire engine in the backyard of the rectory when I first went to visit. It disappeared before I moved in, but the first Saturday I was in the parish, a fire broke out somewhere uptown. Colman said to me, "Do you want to come with me to a fire?" I wasn't crazy about going, but I politely said, "Okay, I'll go." We got into his car and sped to the fire. It was in an apartment building mainly for senior citizens, but it was not serious. Colman was in his glory shaking hands with the firefighters and the seniors in the building. I came to find out that he had in his sitting room every sort of emergency radio equipment so he could monitor the emergencies in the city, and his walls were lined with hundreds of toy fire engines. That was the last fire I attended unless there was a need for my presence. Who would have guessed that I would be appointed chaplain to the Bergen County Fire Department two years later?

If I enjoyed St. Luke's so much and loved the parishioners, why did I ask out of the parish after one year? The answer is multi-faceted. While I was the associate pastor of the parish, I felt that I was not part of the parish staff and leadership. Father Thomas O'Byrne had been the weekend assistant for many years, and he and Father Colman Finneran were the closest of friends. Unfortunately, Colman allowed Tom O'Byrne to make decisions for the parish without consulting the staff, including me. Colman, Tom O'Byrne, and a parish worker formed the St. Luke's "threesome" who had a lot to say about what went on in the parish.

One of the crucial issues the parish was confronted with was its music ministry. Music was not a priority especially during Sunday and Holy Day Masses. During my first Christmas in the parish, the music minister showed up for the Christmas Eve Mass, which was celebrated before midnight, but we had no Christmas music on Christmas Day. I was dumbfounded. I asked Colman, "Why isn't there music today?" He told me that the musicians were tired and wanted to be with their families on Christmas Day. I thought to myself, *I would like to be with my family on Christmas Day, too, but I have other responsibilities.*

St. Luke's was one of the only parishes in the archdiocese to have a Sunday evening Mass, which I enjoyed thoroughly. It usually attracted young people, and many expressed their appreciation for my homilies. They also loved the guitar music that was played at that Mass. However, one never knew if the guitar musician would show up. He came when he wanted and didn't when he didn't want to. If I knew I was to preside at that Mass, I would phone the musician and remind him to show up, but that didn't work very often, either. Music is critical at Catholic (and other faiths') liturgies, and not having music left me with a very bad taste in my mouth.

The most distressing aspect of Colman Finneran's and the threesomes' leadership was an organization they founded that belied any semblance of propriety and class. Father Colman Finneran, Father Tom O'Byrne, other church workers, and I used to gather in the rectory dining room between Sunday Masses to read the newspapers, eat breakfast, and talk. My first Sunday there, I had a hard time comprehending what they were talking about. They kept referring to the "FARTS," which stood for the Fraternal Association of Rectory Trouble Shooters. At first, I thought they were kidding, but it was no joke.

Every now and then, the priests and another church worker invited some of the men of the parish on Saturday nights to the rectory for cigars and drinks. I had to leave every time they met due to my allergy. I couldn't return to my own rooms until well after midnight when they met. The men drank and smoked excessively, told loud and raucous stories and jokes, and left the rectory smelling like a saloon. I couldn't believe that two priests and a music director would assemble a society known as the "FARTS." I think many of them thought I was a prude, but my idea of priesthood was not that.

When Archbishop McCarrick assigned the newly ordained to their parishes, he announced he was also appointing veteran priests to each of us as our mentors. Assigned to me was Father Donald Regan, pastor of a parish in Bergen County. Almost from the beginning of our monthly meetings, I expressed that I couldn't believe that priests and Church employees would assemble a society known as the "FARTS." Father Regan found it hard to believe that such a group existed and advised me to stay away. Each month, we met at a local restaurant for lunch, and I always had another issue to discuss. Father Donald Regan was a tall man who was connected rather tightly with some of the archdiocesan insiders. He took his role as a mentor seriously, which I appreciated greatly.

One of the issues I discussed with Donald Regan was the rectory cook. I am neither fussy nor demanding about cooks and/or food. I was in the religious life for twenty-three years, and much of the time, we religious brothers cooked for ourselves. Needless to say, having a cook in the priesthood was a perk, but the cook at St. Luke's had a distinct way about her. She was a tall, full-bodied woman who lived in an apartment near the local park. She and I quickly locked horns.

The cook had a sign-in sheet on the refrigerator for the priests to either sign in or out for dinner. I was unaware of the sign-in sheet since I had just moved in, and I showed up in the dining room one evening for dinner. Suddenly, the swinging door connecting the kitchen and dining room was violently swung into the dining room, and the cook pointed at me, yelling, "Hey, you, the next time you don't sign in for dinner, you ain't eatin'."

Father Colman was there as well. I turned to him and said, "Colman, I know she's not speaking to me, because no one speaks to me that way." Colman turned red and flustered and said to me, "Bob, don't worry, I will handle her." He then went into the kitchen and spoke to the cook, telling her something I could not hear.

Another time, I showed up for lunch, which was served to the entire staff, including the parish secretaries (except one, who thought it was not healthy to eat in our kitchen) and the housekeepers. I sat down at the kitchen table with the women, all of whom were great in so many ways, and the cook brought me a bowl of soup. I said, "Thank you," and as she walked away, I said, "Excuse me, may I have a soup spoon, please?" Something unimaginable then occurred. She said, "Sure, here you go," and reached into her bosom and pulled out a soup spoon, which she handed to me. Those at the table were astonished as well, and I am not sure I ate the soup that day. While at St. Luke's, I ate out much more often than I ate in for obvious reasons.

As my first year of priesthood continued, it became clear that I might have to move elsewhere. But two very serious incidents made it imperative that I ask for a transfer. While the pastor, Father Colman Finneran, was on vacation for a month in July, 1998, I was supposed to be in charge since I was the next in line of authority, but Father Tom O'Byrne showed up almost every day, renovating an apartment for himself above the kitchen and garage. One parish staff member referred to Tom as "King Thomas" because of the deference paid to him by Colman Finneran.

The pastor's vacation involved him taking a Greyhound bus to Roswell, New Mexico, to look for the aliens. Yes, I am serious. I am not sure to this day if he was serious or not. He was too frightened to fly, so he took Greyhound buses. He said he loved Greyhounds because he met God's people on the buses, and he loved Roswell, New Mexico, and searching for the aliens.

A woman who spoke broken English came to the rectory in July to lodge a complaint against a school staff member who also spoke broken English. She told me that he had sexually abused her in his workshop in the school building. I told the woman I would follow up on the allegation and get back to her. I then called the school staff member in and asked for his story. He denied it over and over, but I believe there was something going on between them, but I couldn't tell if it was consensual or not. I advised the woman to file a police report if she thought he was abusive, but she did not. I waited until the pastor came back to report it to him. When the pastor came back, I am not sure he investigated anything.

The second serious incident involved a family in the parish that complained that two of their sons had been sexually abused by one of my predecessors, Father Dennis Houlihan. When Father Dennis

Houlihan left St. Luke's, he was named secretary to Archbishop McCarrick. The family's complaint about the sexual abuse was dismissed by everyone to whom they spoke, including a bishop, a priest personnel director, and the pastor, Father Colman Finneran. Mark Crawford and his brother, David, alleged that Father Houlihan sexually abused them on a number of occasions in their home and on various trips. The Crawfords were a large family and very active in the parish. Their two boys were brutally sexually abused. For example, on a train trip to the west, Father Houlihan sexually abused Mark Crawford numerous times.

When Colman Finneran told me about the complaints by the Crawfords, he said to me, "Bob, you might hear rumors in the parish that the Crawford family claimed that their sons were abused by Father Dennis Houlihan. Don't believe them; they are crazy." At the time, Colman Finneran did not know about my own history of sexual abuse, and he wasn't expecting my reaction. My head dropped in sorrow for the family, and I think the pastor was afraid I believed them, which I did. During my time at St. Luke's, I never met any of the Crawfords, but I hoped I would so I could provide my pastoral assistance to them. After that interaction with Colman Finneran, I knew I could not, in good conscience, remain in St. Luke's Parish. Ironically, I came to know Mark and David Crawford. Mark would become a state-wide leader against child abuse.

I discussed all of these issues with my mentor, Father Donald Regan, and he agreed that it might be good for me to ask for a transfer. I then asked Archbishop McCarrick for a transfer, which shocked Father Colman Finneran. He never thought I would ask out after my first year. I could not tell him at that time that the Crawford matter was the straw that broke the camel's back, because I was afraid he would conclude that I, too, was a sexual abuse victim.

Robert M. Hoatson, Ph.D.

CHAPTER NINETEEN

MY FIRST PRIESTLY TRANSFER

When Archbishop McCarrick approved my request for a transfer, I had to deal with the Office of Clergy Personnel, led by Monsignor Howard Pohalski, the priest with whom I'd met when I was thinking of becoming a priest and to whom I had asked, "Has McCarrick stopped sleeping with the seminarians?"

Back then, Monsignor Pohalski had been the Director of Justice Programs for the archdiocese, and I'd met him for lunch in the spring of 1994 at a local Spanish restaurant. I was still a Christian Brother and the Director of Total Parish Education at Sacred Heart Parish in Westchester County. Monsignor Howard had been a religious brother before he became a priest, so Archbishop McCarrick thought it would be good for me to speak to someone who had a similar path to the priesthood as mine.

I actually started the conversation with Monsignor Pohalski by asking that question about McCarrick and his sleeping with the seminarians. I figured I could eliminate that archdiocese as a choice if McCarrick was still acting out sexually with seminarians. There was no way that I would put myself at risk after what I went through. Monsignor Howard assured me that McCarrick had stopped sleeping with seminarians because the papal nuncio[5] and Bishop James McHugh, a New Jersey priest who had been ordained a bishop and served as a bishop in New Jersey and New York before dying at a young age, had ordered him to stop immediately and sell the house at the Jersey Shore where McCarrick slept with the seminarians. McCarrick sold the first house, but he soon purchased another house a few miles further south on the Jersey Shore.

---

5   The pope's representative to the United States

The papal nuncio and Bishop James McHugh, who began as a bishop in New Jersey, supposedly instructed McCarrick to stop his misbehavior. By the time I met with Monsignor Howard Pohalski, I had not been sexually abused since 1982, the last time Brother Martin Francis Connelly abused me in my bedroom at Catholic Memorial High School, and I wasn't about to go through that again. Besides, I was probably too old for McCarrick by then; I was 42.

The rumors about McCarrick's preference for good-looking young men and/or boys spread for decades, emanating from his time as Cardinal Edward Egan's secretary and then as auxiliary bishop of the Archdiocese of New York. McCarrick had a habit of calling many young men his "nephews," but Theodore McCarrick was an only child. He couldn't have nephews, but his favorites often "became" his nephews. One of the most disturbing stories about McCarrick and his possible favorites was his connection with "The Preppy Murder."

Robert Chambers, a tall, handsome young man who attended a series of private schools in Manhattan in which he never fit in, pleaded guilty to the murder of Jennifer Levin, a young woman from a wealthy family who dated Chambers and was killed in Central Park, New York. Robert's mother, a nurse, was born in Ireland and worked for Cardinal Edward Egan. After Robert Chambers was arrested, Archbishop McCarrick wrote a letter vouching for his character and asking for reasonable bail. McCarrick was Robert Chambers' godfather at his baptism, and Robert had been an altar server as a young boy. The question has been asked since the 1986 murder, *Did McCarrick have anything to do with Robert Chambers' difficult life?*

My pursuit of a new assignment began with a mailing from Monsignor Pohalski with a list of parishes that had openings in 1998–1999 for an associate pastor. It was a list of approximately twelve parishes. I was instructed to choose whatever parishes I thought I might like and phone those pastors for interviews. One of the parishes that had an opening was Saint Joseph's Parish, West Orange, New Jersey that I attended years earlier. I informed the pastor that I was highly allergic to cat and dog dander and cigar/cigarette smoke. I was invited for an interview, but I turned the parish down because a priest in the parish owned a dog.

Another parish I interviewed in was another Hudson County parish. It was the kind of parish that I thought I would like because I loved cities. However, the pastor allowed the two secretaries whose offices were in the rectory to smoke, and both were chain smokers. I had to turn that parish down, too. Then I went to a parish in Essex County, which seemed to fit my style as well. Unfortunately, I met the cook who lived in the rectory, and he smoked in the kitchen and in his room in the rectory. He was one of the live-in cooks in the archdiocese.

I interviewed in another Essex County parish that was considered a plum parish because it was located in a fairly wealthy town with a school and lots of property. The pastor was a very popular priest in the archdiocese. He taught for some time at the seminary, and I made an appointment to see him. One of the first things he asked me was, "Why are you asking for a transfer after your first year of priesthood? It isn't prudent to do because you could develop a reputation as being a malcontent." I could not tell him that I left

St. Luke's Parish because of the sexual abuse of the Crawford family and also because I was afraid he would conclude that I was a victim, too. I wasn't ready to admit that yet. He also mentioned that he smoked a cigar in his room after dinner every night, so it wouldn't have worked for me anyway.

I also interviewed at another larger Bergen County parish with a veteran pastor. It was a bulging parish with a high school, elementary school, and a large number of families. It was the only parish in the town. The former convent of the parish housed retired and pedophile priests. I felt the interview went very well, but evidently, the pastor did not ask for me. Interestingly, a credibly accused pedophile priest was assigned to the parish in 1999 and remained there until his death in 2012.

Monsignor Pohalski was baffled I hadn't been placed in a parish, but I told him that many of the rectories would adversely affect my health. That May, 1998, I met Monsignor Pohalski at the cathedral before the ordination ceremony of several more priests. He said to me, "Bob, I haven't been able to find a place for you, but something just opened up. Bishop Sean Scanlon said he would take you at his Bergen County parish." I said, "That sounds great, Howard. Sure, I will go there if the rectory is smoke free and there are no pets." He assured me that both conditions were satisfied. I said, "Fine, when do I start?" He said I would be in the June transfer cycle. I had already known Bishop Scanlon from having lived with him in another parish for a few months before moving into the seminary. I would now be returning to the one-star general army chaplain, who would be my pastor.

It was published in the June, 1998 edition of the diocesan newspaper that I was transferred to a Bergen County parish. Many St. Luke's parishioners were stunned by the news, but I couldn't tell them the basis for the transfer because I wasn't prepared to reveal to them the Crawford sexual abuse by Father Dennis Houlihan and my own history of sexual abuse. The parish gave me a goodbye reception in the rectory, and my own parents attended. My parents really liked Father Colman Finneran because he was "so nice," and they couldn't understand why I was leaving such a comfortable place. It was only years later that I could tell them the whole story.

I arrived at Holy Trinity Parish in Hackensack, New Jersey in June, 1998, but I was never told the truth about why I was transferred there. Monsignor Howard Pohalski, by then the Director of Clergy Personnel, simply told me that there was an opening there and that Bishop Sean Scanlon would be willing to take me. Never did he tell me that I was going there to replace a priest, Alberto Santiago, who was accused of sexually abusing a young male parishioner while the two were on a vacation at a Mexican resort. I had to learn this information from parishioners who pulled me aside one day and asked me if I had heard about Father Alberto. I was furious that nothing was said about why I was assigned to Holy Trinity Parish.

According to parishioners, Father Alberto and the young man, whose family was as connected to the parish as possible since they ran a local business, were in a taxi cab in Cancun, and the priest made a move to "go down" on the young man in the back seat of the taxi. When Father Alberto lowered his head toward the young man's crotch, the young man purportedly reached out his hand-held camera and took a photo of the priest going down on him. I was shown a photo of the assault by parishioners, who couldn't believe Father Alberto had not been removed from the parish long before June, 1998.

It turns out that Father Alberto Santiago was being protected by two bishops who wanted him to remain in the parish; namely, Bishop Sean Scanlon and Bishop Matthew Jarmulowicz. Jarmulowicz trained and mentored Alberto Santiago from the time he was a kid in a parish where Jarmulowicz was pastor. It was commonly known that Jarmulowicz protected Santiago his entire life including after he was allegedly dismissed from Immaculate Conception

Seminary long before he was ordained. Monsignor Carl Devlin, rector, and the seminary faculty had found that then-seminarian Alberto Santiago was not a suitable candidate for the priesthood and dismissed him.

However, the archbishop, McCarrick, supposedly through Bishop Jarmulowicz, overrode the decision of the seminary rector and his faculty and placed Alberto in a different seminary in another state. Had the rector's decision not been overturned, perhaps the young man from Holy Trinity Parish who suffered terrible trauma ever since he was assaulted in a taxi, would not have been abused.

Alberto was eventually ordained a priest for the archdiocese and wound up being assigned to various parishes because there were always "rumblings" about his misbehavior in practically every parish to which he was assigned. His behavior at Holy Trinity Parish created a kerfuffle that reverberated from the offices of the archbishop, to the office of the vicar general, Monsignor Dennis Doyle, to the offices of the auxiliary bishops, Scanlon and Jarmulowicz, and the parish, which was a faithful community and family.

Monsignor Dennis Doyle had been the immediate past pastor of Holy Trinty Parish before being named Vicar General of the archdiocese. He was a very popular and pastoral priest who seemed to be on the path toward becoming a bishop. When the family reported to him, their good friend and pastor, what had happened to their son, Monsignor Doyle immediately began an investigation and believed the young man. He thought Father Alberto should be transferred immediately, according to the abused family and many parishoners. However, Sean Scanlon and Jarmulowicz had the ear of the archbishop, and it appeared that the bishops would get their way. Father Alberto would remain in the parish. When Archbishop McCarrick finally decided to take Monsignor Doyle's advice, Monsignor Doyle likely surrendered his chances at becoming a bishop because the two auxiliary bishops, Scanlon and Jarmulowicz, were furious with him and joined the chorus of some clerics who thought Doyle was the problem.

The way I found out about the identity of the young man and his family was at lunch one of my first days in the rectory. It was June, 1998, and there were three or four of us sitting at the dining room table waiting to be served lunch. Bishop Scanlon was called away for something, so Father Jesus Orlando Rengifo, Father Ben Ippolito, the parish administrator, a seminarian on summer duty, and I began eating. Bishop Scanlon then walked through the dining room with three people who looked like a family. The mood of the bishop and the family was serious, so I didn't bother asking those at the dining room table who they were or why they were there.

About twenty minutes later, the family walked through the dining room, and it was clear that one or more of them was crying or had been crying. Bishop Scanlon then sat at the head of the table while the rest of us were silent. He then said, "I guess I should tell you guys what's happening. That was the McMahon family and they came to see me to let bygones be bygones now that Alberto has been transferred, and they wanted to give me the church donations they had been withholding until Alberto was gone. I told them they can keep their donations because they went after one of my priests, and I said I would not forgive them for what they did."

The bishop mentioned that the three people were Gerald McMahon, the owner of a local business which had extensive dealings with the church, his wife Irene, and their son, Brendan, the alleged victim of the sexual assault by Father Alberto in a Mexican resort. Brendan was in his early twenties at the time. The bishop then told us that he would not be friends with the McMahons because of the hassle they caused with Father Alberto. I was shocked, to say the least, that a bishop, let alone a bishop who was a pastor, would treat a parish family, and especially a parish family that was so closely tied to the parish, in that manner. Then, I nearly lost my lunch when Bishop Scanlon added, "Besides, I sent Alberto for pedophilia testing, and he passed."

First of all, the matter of Father Alberto and Brendan McMahon was not a pedophilic matter. It was an adult-on-adult assault. Sending Father Alberto for pedophilia testing was not necessary. Besides, I hadn't heard of anyone being tested for pedophilia, and the bishop didn't describe how the testing took place. All I knew was that I was replacing a priest accused of sexually abusing a young adult parishioner and was never told anything about it until I arrived.

Father Alberto was transferred to another parish, but he soon ended up as an incardinated priest (meaning he completely changed dioceses) when Bishop Matthew Jarmulowicz was named the bishop of another diocese. Lunch ended in relative silence, and I went to my room (which Alberto occupied until I arrived) to consider what I just witnessed and what I considered scandalous behavior on the bishop's part.

Brendan McMahon was not the only Holy Trinity parishioner Father Santiago attempted to sexually abuse. He asked a parishioner familiar with technology, Ernest Barbato, to repair his computer. When Mr. Barbato finished fixing Fr. Alberto's computer in his sitting room, Fr. Alberto asked him to sit on the couch with him and have a glass of wine. While socializing with Ernest, Father Alberto made a sexual move on him, trying to place a kiss on Ernest's lips. Ernest reported that Father Alberto told him he was a computer science major in college, so it was most likely not to have him fix his computer that Father Alberto had invited him to his suite of rooms.

From that day on, I sensed I had been transferred to yet another parish where sexual abuse was not handled properly or sensitively. I was not aware at the time that we had a pedophile priest on the staff, Father Jesus Orlando Rengifo, who served the Hispanic community, mostly people from his home country. Father Orlando was favored by Bishop Scanlon because he was well liked by the Hispanic community and it was difficult for a pastor to have a full-time, Spanish-speaking priest. Orlando lived next door to me in a suite that was constructed just for him. I lived in a suite of rooms that did not have its own bathroom. I had to use the public bathroom on the second floor for my needs.

Many years later, after Father Orlando went home to South America, an announcement went out from the vicar general of the archdiocese, warning pastors all over the country not to hire Father Orlando as a priest because there were credible allegations of sexual abuse of children against him.

When Father Alberto moved out of Holy Trinity Parish, he took most of the furniture from his suite of rooms, which was not unusual. Diocesan priests often purchased their own furniture and moved it with them wherever they went. Since I was in the religious life for 23 years and owned nothing, my sitting room needed furniture. Instead of allowing me to go shopping to pick out sitting room furniture, the administrator of the parish, Father Ben Ippolito, was instructed by Bishop Scanlon to take the parish credit card and shop with me in a furniture store in another town. He purchased a couch and a couple of end tables, and they were delivered soon after. Imagine a 46-year-old priest not being permitted to shop for furniture for his own room. I said to myself, *Oh my God, not St. Luke's again*, meaning that I was getting the idea that the clerical culture was dysfunctional and juvenile everywhere, not just in Hudson County.

Robert M. Hoatson, Ph.D.

In 2019, Brendan McMahon reported the sexual assault by Father Alberto to the bishop of the diocese where Father Alberto had been accepted and welcomed. Father Alberto was placed on leave of absence. Since then, the clergy of the diocese was informed that Father Alberto was no longer a priest.

In the summer of 2021, Gerald and Irene McMahon's daughter, Dr. Eileen McMahon, a former student of mine from the parish school, was married at a gala affair at a famous and fancy local restaurant. After the wedding and during the early morning hours of the next day, Gerald McMahon suffered a medical emergency and passed away. I believe that the stress and trauma of his son's sexual abuse and his frustration with Church leadership for whom he once had great respect but who clearly were trying to cover it up, led to his demise.

Once I got settled and began to become more active in the parish, I thought I would ask to see Bishop Scanlon to find out how he liked to be addressed. When I lived with him at another parish several years earlier and was a seminarian, I referred to him as Bishop Scanlon on all occasions. I entered his office and asked him if I could ask him a quick question. I asked, "How would you like me to address you, Bishop?" He seemed a bit taken aback by my question because I sensed that he wanted to say, "Bishop would be fine." He stuttered through the following: "My name is Sean." He never expressed whether or not he wanted to be called that, so I called him "Bishop" my entire time there.

The parish was a super-busy parish, which was right up my alley. There were three daily Masses, one Saturday evening Mass, and four Masses on Sunday. There was a host of funerals and many weddings, mostly because of the gorgeous church and its long, main aisle. The parish had a school that was floundering but still in operation in a large, beautifully built building across the street. I said to myself, *I think I'll like it here.* And I did, for two years. My duties included being the chaplain of the youth group, Pre-Cana, the scouts, and the Hackensack Fire Department, besides the duties of being full-time associate pastor and taking "duty" a few days per week.

"Duty" was largely an antiquated practice whereby a priest would be assigned daily to respond to emergencies and other parish business. Bishop Scanlon insisted that the "duty" priest be in the rectory while on duty, but it made no sense, since a "duty" priest could be contacted in a matter of a few seconds through his personal cell phone. Most parishes no longer had duty, and my previous assignment in Hudson County did not have a duty policy. In fact, my first emergency call in the peninsula parish occurred at 3:00 a.m. the first Saturday I was there. It was the local police department calling. I picked up the rectory phone and said, "Good evening, St. Luke's." The voice on the other end said, "Good morning, Father, this is the Hudson County Police Department calling. We have an emergency uptown in an apartment building, and the family would like a member anointed. The address is not in your parish, Father, it's in Saint Peter's Parish, but those priests never answer the phone." I said, "I will be right there."

My first anointing was of a man whose body was lying on the kitchen table on a mattress because there was no room for his bed. He and his brother had collected so many newspapers and junk that one could barely move in the apartment. It reminded me of the Collyer brothers story from Manhattan, who had hoarded so much junk that the junk killed them. Something told me that the junk in the apartment killed that man, too. In any case, St. Luke's Parish responded to duty when the priests at St. Peter's should have responded to it.

Robert M. Hoatson, Ph.D.

I was the only priest at Holy Trinity Parish who followed the duty policy. Father Orlando was out all the time and never followed the duty schedule. Father Ben Ippolito, the parish administrator, had lots of priest friends, and he went out on his duty days as well. In fact, he tried at one time to switch duty with me on my day off, but I had made plans. He didn't leave me a note until I was leaving for my day off, so I didn't bother responding. I did not believe it was fair that he asked me to switch with him so late in the day.

When I returned from my day off, I was screamed at by Bishop Scanlon and Father Ippolito for not being on duty when Ippolito had asked me. I concluded that the entire scenario was staged to see if I deferred to them in taking duty. It was then that I decided to do what I had to do in the parish and ignore the two of them. I even stopped eating in the rectory because I didn't want to break bread with fakers. I alerted the cook, who was fantastic, that it was not because of her food (which was professionally prepared, by the way) that I would not be eating any longer in the rectory, but because I couldn't stand being around the priests. She understood.

A month or so into my time at Holy Trinity Parish, I unknowingly began to dig my grave because of our first staff meeting. I was happy to hear that Holy Trinity conducted staff meetings, and all of us were asked to submit items for the agenda. Foolishly and probably naively, I thought the request for agenda items was a serious attempt to talk about the parish, its growth, and improvement. I submitted seven or eight items, including a request for a clarification of the job descriptions of some of the parish workers.

During the first funeral at which I presided at Holy Trinty, one of the workers wanted to train me on how funerals were conducted there. I was confused because the parish had a liturgy coordinator, but it soon became obvious that some workers were "in" with the bishop and others were not. Bishop Scanlon had a couple of "deep throats" who reported everything to him. To my amazement, one of the workers sat in the last pew of the church during the entire funeral. He didn't seem to be cleaning or repairing anything. I asked at the staff meeting if one of the workers was in charge of funerals. Silence came over the room. No one said anything except Bishop Scanlon, who didn't answer my question; rather, he defended that one particular worker. I found it peculiar that he knew who I was referring to, when I hadn't mentioned any one particular worker's name. It must have been his guilty conscience.

It was that one worker who reported everything to the bishop on a regular basis, spending more time in the bishop's office than most other members did combined. He did whatever the bishop ordered him to do, including spying on the staff, especially the clergy. I shied away from that person and most of the staff members because the parish appeared to be severely dysfunctional. The bishop had a secretary, who was paid for being his secretary, but she also took a salary for being Director of Religious Education. She also was in charge of collecting the school tuition, which was largely left to me to collect as principal of the school. She, "Deep Throat," and the bishop were peas in a pod, and the information cycle passed through those three persons. The clergy had little to nothing to say about any matters.

Just before the parish school year started in September, 1999, the current principal was hired at one of the top public elementary schools in the state. Since I had significant experience as a Catholic school educator and principal, Bishop Scanlon asked me to become principal of the parish school. I wondered where his request came from, since he was not very fond of me. It appears that a Sister of Charity, who had been at the parish for several decades and had been the parish school principal decades ago, put the bug in the bishop's ear to ask me to be principal. When the bishop asked me, he told me he would relieve me of some other duties in the parish so I could get a day off.

I told the pastor I would be the principal, and I came to understand that the school's enrollment had dropped significantly through the years. There were only 200 students in grades K-8, and the usual "magic" number for a school being kept open in the archdiocese was 225 students. I began to work on the enrollment, and it shot up almost 165 students to a total of nearly 365 students. I also rented an office and two classrooms to a private school for autistic children, which brought in revenue. I started two Pre-K classes for ages 3 and 4 as well. Our Spanish-speaking families began to enroll their children en masse because they wanted their children to have a Catholic education, and Father Orlando promised me that he and his community would raise money to help pay for many of the tuitions. I had a weekly column in the Sunday bulletin and kept the parishioners up to date regarding honor rolls, renovations, enrollments, service projects by the students, and many other activities. The parishioners were thrilled that their parish had a Catholic school.

Despite his promise to do so, Bishop Scanlon had not taken any responsibilities away from me and working seven days a week began to weigh on me. My schedule did not allow for a day off. By this time, I was in my second year as principal and was tired from all the ministries of which I was in charge.

Therefore, at a staff meeting where the new administrator, Father Philip Concannon, was present, I asked the bishop to relieve me of my youth ministry work since the youth group for high school students met on Sunday evenings. I told him that if I were relieved of that role, I could preside at Sunday morning Masses and then take off for a half day of rest and relaxation.

When he heard my request, Bishop Scanlon angrily responded, "Bob, you are the youth minister." I then reminded him that he had promised to take some responsibilities from me after taking on the role of the principal so I could have a day off. He repeated, "You are the youth minister." Finally, I pushed my right to have a day off, and he very angrily answered me, "Bob, you are the youth minister, and if you don't like it, go down to the archbishop and get a transfer."

Father Concannon said nothing at the meeting in my defense, nor did Father Orlando who also attended the meeting. To make matters worse, that Christmas, Bishop Scanlon gave me the same $75 gift that he gave everyone else after I saved the parish at least $60,000 by being the unpaid principal of the school and the unpaid youth minister. I was insulted and felt like handing the card back to him. *What a cheap Charlie,* I said to myself.

I took the bishop up on his offer and threat. I made an appointment with Archbishop McCarrick and asked for a transfer. I told him about Bishop Scanlon and his unreasonable "slave" mentality, and McCarrick expressed his disappointment because he said I was doing invaluable work at the parish. I told him that I performed 30 of the 50 weddings that year, presided at most of the funerals, and was responsible for the parish school and all the other activities. I told him I needed a day off each week. He then asked, "Bobby, what do you want to do next, and where do you want to live?" I told him I thought I would love to remain in education. He said, "Fine. I would like you to work with our superintendent of schools so you can become an assistant superintendent."

I made an appointment to see the superintendent, a Sister of Charity whom I knew fairly well from having worked in a large archdiocese for many years. She was principal of an all-girls high school when I was stationed a few blocks away at an all-boys school. The two schools merged in the early 1980s and then closed in the middle 2000s. The sister became the associate superintendent of secondary schools for the archdiocese. She and I studied at Fordham University for our doctoral degrees.

When I interviewed with the superintendent, she asked me if I would be comfortable with an assistant superintendent's position, which entailed the raising of significant funds for inner-city schools of the archdiocese. She recalled that I was the founder of Catholic Urban Educators of America while I was at Fordham University and was essentially running the office of non-public education. My mentor, Dr. Robert J. Starratt, SJ, a noted educational scholar, was the titular head of the office, but he was in the process of leaving his religious order at the time in order to marry.

I was Dr. Starratt's graduate assistant, and he had great plans for C.U.E., a national network of Catholic Urban Educational administrators and teachers. He handed over the organization to me while I finished my doctorate, and the office secretary and I ran the office and C.U.E. successfully for a couple of years. We held national conferences in New York, Chicago, and Los Angeles and directed those conferences toward underserved populations of Catholics, especially African-Americans and Hispanics. The superintendent of schools thought I would be perfect for such a position, and we planned on my taking that position in June, 2001.

Just as I was preparing to move into the office of Catholic education, Archbishop McCarrick was named Archbishop of Washington, DC, and Bishop Matthew Jarmulowicz, my nemesis, was named interim archbishop of my archdiocese, Newark, New Jersey.

CHAPTER TWENTY

BUS ACCIDENT

I was not a favorite of Bishop Matthew Jarmulowicz since I had just moved out of the parish where his good friend Bishop Sean Scanlon was pastor, and I complained about him to Archbishop McCarrick. Keep in mind those two bishops protested Father Alberto Santiago's transfer from Holy Trinity Parish. I didn't have a snowball's chance in hell because Bishop Jarmulowicz's other close friend was Director of Clergy Personnel, Monsignor Howard Pohalski. Both men, Jarmulowicz and Pohalski, called me into the office of the interim Archbishop of Newark.

Bishop Jarmulowicz informed me that I would *not* be named Associate Superintendent of Schools because he was making cuts in archdiocesan personnel. I am not sure he was telling me the whole truth because he made almost no cutbacks in the archdiocese while he was interim archbishop. In fact, an interim archbishop is not supposed to make too many changes because those changes should be left to the newly appointed archbishop, whoever that is to be. I did not react since I knew he had it out for me. He and Monsignor Pohalski then told me there was an opening in Our Lady of Good Counsel Parish in Newark for a Director of Schools since the pastor, Monsignor Joseph Plunkett, no longer felt he could manage the schools and the parish.

Our Lady of Good Counsel Parish had been a large German and Irish parish in the north ward of Newark that transitioned in the 1990s to a nearly exclusive Hispanic parish with Cubans, Dominicans, and Puerto Ricans predominating. The high school was in crisis because of poor facilities and weak leadership. The high school enrollment was made up of mostly African-American and Latino families who believed Our Lady of Good Counsel was a better option than the Newark public secondary schools, which were perceived as violent and academically poor. The elementary school was primarily Hispanic and in much better condition. I told Bishop Jarmulowicz and Monsignor Pohalski I would be happy to go to Our Lady of Good Counsel.

On the way out of our meeting, Bishop Jarmulowicz and I shared an elevator. Just as we were getting on the elevator, he turned to me and nastily commented, "Bob, you really haven't given parish life a chance, have you?" I responded, "Excuse me, Bishop, but I have spent the past four years in parishes, and I was deeply involved in both, including being principal of Holy Trinity School." Jarmulowicz sensed my annoyance and responded, "Oh, I guess you did give parish life a chance." We exited the elevator, and I thought to myself, *You arrogant son of a bitch.*

I made an appointment to meet with the pastor of Our Lady of Good Counsel Parish (most often called Good Counsel), Monsignor Joseph Plunkett. We met at a Spanish restaurant on the Newark/Belleville line, right off Branch Brook Park. It was a pleasant place to have a meeting, and it was obvious that Joe Plunkett was a very nice man. During our dinner, Joe admitted that he no longer wanted anything to do with the schools of the parish because of the deep problems that existed, especially in the high school.

He said the high school was largely in chaos, but the elementary school was in decent shape. It was led by Mr. Jason Callahan whose family I knew from my hometown and whose brother, Tom, was in my class at Essex Catholic High School. Jason also graduated from Essex Catholic. Monsignor Plunkett claimed that the main high school building, one of two very old structures, was scheduled for a gutting and major renovation in the summer of 2001. He said Mrs. Gladys Ramos was the principal of the high school but was not a very strong leader. She is a Filipina woman whose administrative skills were lacking, and she essentially relied on two Sisters of Saint Joseph for advice and counsel.

After we spoke at length about the schools, Monsignor Plunkett asked me where I was going to live. I said I assumed I would live in the rectory of Our Lady of Good Counsel. He then asked, "Do you speak Spanish?" I said, "No, but I do speak French." I said it in jest because I knew the parish was nearly exclusively Spanish-speaking. Monsignor Plunkett then advised that I not live in the Good Counsel rectory because nearly all of the interactions in the rectory were conducted in Spanish, including speaking to the cook, housekeeper, and committees of the parish. I said, "Okay, I'll let 'downtown' know about that and see if they want to assign me to another rectory."

In the meantime, I happened to be speaking to the woman from the archdiocese who handles finances for the parishes, Helen Nash, who informed me that there may be an opening for a priest to live at Our Lady of Lourdes rectory in my hometown. Her nephew was working in the parish that summer and was hired by the pastor, Father Joseph Petrillo. I contacted Father Joseph and asked to see him. Joseph Petrillo and I met at the rectory, and he showed me a room on the second floor. The floor had been divided rather strangely into two suites at the front of the house, but Joseph said he would change things around if I wanted to move in. I asked him to switch my suite of rooms so I could have a contiguous bathroom, and his suite of rooms was moved entirely across the hall. I was very appreciative and thanked Father Joseph for being so open to having me live there.

Once again, I thought I was moving into a peaceful and functional rectory and parish. I said Masses in the parish, and I knew some of the parishioners from having lived in the same town for years growing up. I also became a weekend assistant at St. Catharine's Parish, Glen Rock, New Jersey; St. Timothy's Parish, Closter, New Jersey, and Nativity Parish, Midland Park, New Jersey. I worked all week at Good Counsel Schools, took Saturdays off, and worked on Sundays in two other parishes.

I was in my glory because I loved to say Mass. I used to tell friends of mine that an exceptional Catholic Mass is more powerful and poignant than the best Broadway musical. Joseph Petrillo treated me well for the first year or so, but things went downhill quickly. First of all, Father Joseph did not like the cook, Sister St. Bernadette, a Franciscan sister, who had lived in the rectory in a room off the kitchen for many years. He made it untenable for her to stay, so she moved out within the year. Father Alexander Smith, a newly ordained priest, was then assigned to the parish, and was well-liked by some parishioners, but his path and mine rarely crossed.

Father Alexander Smith was a favorite of the new archbishop, John J. Myers, who had arrived in 2001, and Father Alexander quickly rose through the ranks. He became the vocation director and chaplain at a local college, where he continues to work. After taking some time off from the priesthood for personal reasons, Alexander Smith returned as chaplain of the local college. Shortly thereafter, he was named head of the university apostolate.

Father Joseph Petrillo hired one woman to be the new cook and housekeeper, and she nearly burned down the kitchen and forgot to do my laundry on several occasions. She was a nice lady, but she hadn't a clue. She left in due time, and I told Joseph that I preferred to do my own laundry and get my own meals since I missed many meals because of my work at Our Lady of Good Counsel in Newark. Besides, Joseph Petrillo was an entertainer, and it wasn't unusual to find a dining room table full of nuns or priests when I came home from school.

Joseph loved nuns, and he loved cooking for nuns. He was stationed in a few schools, so he got to know lots of nuns, mainly the Felician Sisters and Sisters of Charity. He was also friendly with some priests who were less than holy, pious, and pastoral. One of his friends sexually abused a classmate of mine; another was known for having sex with younger men; a third was Father Joseph's best friend, Monsignor Peter Cheplic, who would move into our rectory several months later and force me to move out.

Thankfully, I left the rectory of Our Lady of Lourdes each morning by 6:30 so I could get to the Our Lady of Good Counsel Schools and greet the students. I stood outside most days and said hello to the faculty, staff, and students. The kids were a joy, for the most part. It was my first experience of greeting students from kindergarten to grade twelve. I had spent the entire summer of 1999 working to get the newly renovated high school building ready for occupancy, and we just made it. We were moving furniture into the high school building on the morning of the first day of classes. I was told by Bishop Jarmulowicz when I took the job that I wouldn't be able to take vacation that summer because I would have to manage the renovation of the high school building and get both schools ready for September.

Once September, 1999, came and went, it was clear to me that the high school needed new leadership. The high school reminded me of the novel *Up the Down Staircase*, in which the school was run by the students, not the adults, and good teachers were becoming more and more disillusioned. I never experienced a Catholic school where students talked back to teachers using swear words and treated the principal and the office staff with abject disrespect.

The straw that broke the camel's back was an accident outside the school involving a school bus and a second grader. The second grader was supposed to be supervised by her high school sister, but she was more interested in flirting with her boyfriend. When I was called to the emergency, I ran from the rectory to the street outside the high school and found that Mrs. Ramos had no teacher assigned to supervise dismissal. In fact, all Mrs. Ramos had to do was walk about fifteen feet to the school entrance and be vigilant about the dismissal behavior of the students. Fortunately, the second grader was not seriously injured, but I knew that a student or staff member would be seriously injured eventually if something was not done.

I am not certain if I entered Mrs. Ramos' office right after the incident or waited until the next morning, but I did ask for her resignation. She answered immediately, "No problem, Father, you can have my resignation." It was as if she knew what was coming and was relieved to no longer be the principal of Our Lady of Good Counsel High School. I thanked her for her service and wished her well. I informed Monsignor Plunkett about her resignation, and I think he was relieved as well.

Just before I arrived at Our Lady of Good Counsel in May, 2001 to tour the parish, I was told by Monsignor Plunkett that Mrs. Ramos had hired a new assistant principal, Mr. Andrew Van Houten. I asked him if it was the same Mr. Andrew Van Houten who had been a Christian Brother, the same religious order I belonged to for 23 years. He said, "Yes, he is the former principal of an upstate New York Catholic high school and a school administrator at a number of other Catholic institutions." I knew Andrew to be a strong educator and administrator, and I hoped he could have a strong influence in the high school. However, he agreed with me that Gladys Ramos had to go, so I asked him if he would take over as principal. He agreed, and the school began to improve immediately.

My one hesitancy about hiring Mr. Van Houten as the new principal was an aspect of his personality I had heard strong rumors about in the Christian Brothers, but I could not confirm those rumors. However, my concern would become a crisis in the near future.

Mr. Van Houten, in turn, named Mr. Harry Hart as assistant principal, a great hire. Harry had taught and coached with me at

Blessed Sacrament High School in New Rochelle, New York in the 1970s, and was a Division I Women's basketball coach at Columba College. He had left Columba College, so I invited him to come to Our Lady of Good Counsel to teach and coach when I took the job there. Harry was one of the finest men and educators I have ever met.

Harry jumped at the offer, despite being a resident of New York City and having to make an hour trip each way. I knew the kids would love him, and they did. I had heard that the basketball coach at the time was recruiting kids to play basketball, but they were not students at all. I asked that coach to step aside because I wanted our coaches to be teachers in the school if at all possible. I also had to ask one of the student-players to leave because he had failed nearly every subject. Harry Hart is African-American, and he was a particularly excellent role model for the boys, although the girls took to him, too.

Mr. Van Houten and Mr. Hart worked together to get the high school in order. They hired a religious sister, Sister Joan Ruth Whittle, a Fanciscan Sister of Peace, who came with a wealth of experience as a teacher, administrator, campus minister, and all-around positive influence. They also hired Mrs. Ania Jarmulowicz (no relation to the bishop), a Polish native who was a whiz at computer science. She inspired her students in no time and eventually became assistant principal of the school after a serious incident concerning Mr. Van Houten. The high school was coming together both academically and discipline-wise. In the meantime, I had to deal with a problem in the elementary school.

The principal of the elementary school, Mr. Jason Callahan, refused to acknowledge that I was assigned to the parish as Director of Schools, not just the director of the high school. He told the faculty of the elementary school that I would have nothing to do with the elementary school, so I had to set him straight. My conversation with him went fairly well, but he continued to ride like a lone ranger, ignoring my memos and not being a team player. Mr. Callahan had appointed an assistant principal for the elementary school without consulting me, and I let him know how I felt about it.

As best as I could calculate, when I carefully examined the "books" of both schools, the subsidy from the archdiocese had kept rising until it had reached $300,000 the year before I arrived. In my first year as director, our subsidy dropped to $100,000 because our administrators and I paid much greater attention to the bills, the salaries, and the tuition payments. Monsignor Plunkett himself had been away from the parish for a couple of years, but before I arrived in 1999 he had already been back for a year or two.

Monsignor Plunkett admitted to me that he was back at Our Lady of Good Counsel because there were problems with administration of the schools and parish. Evidently, a member of the parish clergy had purchased himself an expensive car and charged it to the elementary school. In addition, there were accusations that neglect of the entire parish operation was rampant, and finances were not properly managed. That priest was transferred to another parish, and I made sure the automobile that was purchased did not appear on the school's budget.

Father Plunkett's predecessor had to be removed. Allegedly, he had a substance abuse problem other than alcohol, and there may have been drug sales taking place from the rectory. Besides that, that same priest used many thousands of dollars of school money to purchase himself a Jeep. I made sure that that outlay did not appear on our balance sheet, and I asked if a lot more money than that disappeared from the schools to feed that priest's lifestyle. I was informed that he was appointed pastor of another parish, and he was removed from that parish, too, after thousands of dollars went missing. You would have thought the archdiocese would have learned its lesson, but they moved him to an even larger parish, and he was removed from there, too. He was then placed in a home for priests. When a priest is entangled in a money scandal, the church responds immediately. When a priest is credibly accused of sexually abusing a child, he is treated like an injured puppy.

Because Our Lady of Good Counsel Schools were subsidized by the archdiocese, the financial persons from headquarters came to the rectory monthly to meet with both principals, me, and occasionally the pastor. Helen Nash and the religious sister who was in charge of elementary school finances were less than cordial toward us, blaming us for not collecting enough tuition and not doing enough to raise our revenues. I hated the fact that our principals and I, who were working assiduously to straighten out the finances, were not given even one or two months to make a significant difference. I was so angry with the meetings that I wrote to the archdiocesan education office, asking them to tone down the meetings and give greater thanks and motivation to our principals. That letter was the beginning of my downfall at Our Lady of Good Counsel, since I dared to question archdiocesan personnel.

After my first year at Our Lady of Good Counsel, the elementary school principal, Mr. Jason Callahan, submitted his resignation, which did not surprise me. He did not like that I was his supervisor, so he got a job in another archdiocesan elementary school. We assembled a search committee for his replacement, and Mr. Van Houten had mentioned to me that a very good friend of his, Pat McGrath, was retiring from her New York City public school teaching position and might like to be principal of Our Lady of Good Counsel Elementary School. We interviewed several candidates, but Pat McGrath was, by far, much more experienced and qualified. She taught elementary school subjects for years and was an administrator at a private school in Brooklyn. She was a lifelong Catholic, very active in her parish in Brooklyn, and she expressed her willingness to make the trip from Brooklyn to Newark every day.

Robert M. Hoatson, Ph.D.

What a find Pat McGrath was. Like Harry Hart in the high school, she was a role model for the staff and student body of the elementary school. She and Andrew Van Houten worked closely together to create a one-school type of community despite the two-school structure. They made sure the two schools prayed together and the high school kids helped the younger kids in a number of activities, including mentoring and tutoring. Things were coming together quickly because of the outstanding leadership of Pat McGrath, Andrew Van Houten, and Harry Hart, the schools' administrators. I was feeling confident that Our Lady of Good Counsel Parish had two schools to be proud of and were operating well when two incidents arose that not only forced another change in my residence, but also a major change in the schools of Our Lady of Good Counsel Parish.

CHAPTER TWENTY-ONE

NO PLACE TO GO

I had been living at Our Lady of Lourdes rectory in my hometown for a little over a year when the pastor came into my sitting room one evening as soon as I came home from school. Father Joseph Petrillo often liked to talk, so I thought he might want to know how my day was. He then said, "Bob, may I sit? I need to tell you something." I said, "Sure, Joseph, what's up?" Without hesitating, he let me know, "Bob, I am going to be moving Peter Cheplic into our rectory. He can use the room across the hall." I asked him why, since Monsignor Peter Cheplic was pastor of Saint Aloysius Parish in Hudson County. Father Joseph continued, "Peter has admitted that he sexually abused a minor back in the 1970s, but he assures me that it was only once and that he feels terrible about it."

Somewhat astonished, I said to Joseph, "You can't move a credibly accused pedophile into a rectory. The archdiocesan policy says a credibly accused priest must be moved out of church buildings and placed in safe and monitored places. Besides, Joseph, there is an elementary school about 200 yards from the room where Peter would be living. I would not move him in if I were you." Joseph was surprised that I was against the move, I think, and he said, "Bob, the least we can do is give a brother priest safe haven." I once again told Joseph that it was not a good idea, but he apparently had his mind made up because Peter Cheplic did move in directly across the hall from my room. As a result, I ended up in the emergency room with a serious case of gastritis, indicating my nerves were acting up. I made an appointment with my therapist, who put an end to my gastritis by asking me what I wanted to do. I told him I did not want to live with a pedophile priest, and Dr. William Richardson calmly counseled, "Then move out." He put into words what I was burying in my stomach—that I would not live with a credibly accused pedophile priest.

I made an appointment to see Bishop Arthur Serratelli, the Vicar General of the Archdiocese and I said to him, "Bishop, do you know that Peter Cheplic has been moved into my rectory?" His answer startled me. Without blinking, he said to me, "Oh, that poor man, what he's been through." I think my jaw dropped, realizing that he was more concerned about Peter Cheplic, a self-admitted pedophile priest, than myself or anyone else. I reminded him that Our Lady of Lourdes had an elementary school on the grounds, but that didn't move Serratelli at all. He then asked me a few general questions about what I knew about clergy sexual abuse, my advocacy in Boston, the *Boston Globe* exposition, and how to handle cases. I gave him my best advice and experience, but I could tell it went in one ear and out the other.

I then said, "Bishop, I cannot live in a rectory with a pedophile priest." "Okay," he said, "then you move out. Why not find an acceptable place to live, and let me know what you find." He was as cold and callous as one can get. I began looking for a place to live. When I returned to Our Lady of Good Counsel Schools after my meeting with Bishop Serratelli, I told the administrators of the schools that I would be moving out of Our Lady of Lourdes rectory because Monsignor Peter Cheplic was allowed to move in. By the way, within a few months, I found at least one more victim of Peter Cheplic, and the number of victims was between four and six that we knew of. Mr. Van Houten came to me later on that day with a proposal for a living situation.

Andrew Van Houten lived in the rectory of Saint Timothy's Parish, Closter, New Jersey, practically the last parish in the northeast section of the archdiocese near the Hudson River. Mr. Van Houten was hired in the parish to be the Director of Religious Education when he took a leave of absence from the Christian Brothers. When he was hired at Our Lady of Good Counsel

Schools, he remained Director of Religious Education on weekends at St. Timothy's and continued to live in the rectory there. He suggested I meet with the pastor, Father Dan O'Herlihy.

I met with Father O'Herlihy, and he agreed that I could move into St. Timothy's rectory. Around this time, the bishop of a midwestern diocese, John J. Myers, had been announced as the new archbishop of Newark, and Father Dan O'Herlihy had stopped by my office a few days earlier at Our Lady of Good Counsel to talk about my moving in and to tell me that Myers was rumored to be the next archbishop of Newark. It was distressing to me because I had been following the career of Bishop Myers in Peoria, Illinois, and he was a mean-spirited, ultra-right autocrat. The *National Catholic Reporter* published several stories about Myers, and they were not complimentary. He fired teachers who announced that they were gay, and he clearly opposed homosexuals teaching in Catholic schools. I had a premonition around 1985 that I would have to stand up someday to John J. Myers. I was typing my doctoral dissertation in the Christian Brothers residence in Hell's Kitchen, New York, and picked up a copy of the *National Catholic Reporter*. There was another article about Bishop Myers, who was acting dictatorial in his diocese, Peoria, Illinois, and bragging that he was recruiting vocations in large numbers. It was then that the premonition came to me: someday, I would have to stand up to this man. Who would have thought that six years later, I would be standing up to Archbishop John J. Myers?

I received permission to move into the rectory at St. Timothy's in Closter, New Jersey, and I also began to say Masses on weekdays and weekends. In fact, I said the 6:00 a.m. mass every weekday for the nuns in the parish and then left for school in Essex County. I wasn't at St. Timothy's for more than a few weeks when one of the nuns asked to speak with me. There were five nuns in the parish, four from one religious order and one from another religious order. All taught or worked in the parish elementary school. The nun who asked to see me was the youngest in the convent. I asked her if the front parlor of the rectory would be a good spot to talk. She said, "Yes, that would be great."

She began to tell me a story of abuse in the convent by the superior. The abuse was not sexual; rather, it was abuse of power and authority. This nun said she taught a full schedule in the school, had to cook dinner for the nuns every evening, taught religious education classes after school, and had cleaning duties in the convent as well. She said the superior assigned these tasks, but hardly did anything herself. I advised Sister to contact her religious superiors in Pennsylvania and report the superior, who also was the school principal. She said she couldn't do that because of fear of retaliation. I volunteered to speak to the religious leaders myself, but she asked me not to.

I left the matter alone until all the other nuns in the convent asked to speak to me about the same nun. First of all, the superior/principal almost never attended the morning Mass with the other nuns. They could not understand why, except that she felt she could determine her own schedule. In addition, she had her own car. It was common for a religious order of nuns to have a community car purchased by the parish. I asked each nun to report Sister Superior, but all felt that they would be retaliated against. I didn't realize that I would be harassed and retaliated against also.

Father Dan O'Herlihy, pastor, noticed that the nuns were coming to the rectory to speak to me regularly, and he and the Sister Superior protected each other. The pastor began to retaliate against me for speaking to the nuns by cutting my Mass schedule, giving my rectory garage to the Sister Superior, and admonishing me for bad habits I had, like not putting the sections of the Sunday newspaper back in order after reading them. I began to understand that the pastor was severely dysfunctional and that the Sister Superior was the same. I wrote a letter to the head of the sisters' religious order to inform her of the complaints by all the sisters who lived in the convent. She wrote back and told me to mind my own business.

Since I couldn't get anywhere with the leader of the religious order, I wrote to the Vicar for Religious of the archdiocese, a Dominican nun whose job was to supervise the religious orders that served in the archdiocese. She told me it was an internal community matter with the nuns, and she did nothing. Then, I wrote to the Vicar for Priests and told him about the nuns and the retaliation by the pastor against me. He didn't do anything, either. I knew my days at Saint Timothy's were numbered. The pastor's sister was the cook in the parish, and the housekeeper was his niece.

Father Dan O'Herlihy was a reformed alcoholic who was really a dry drunk because he did nothing about his temper and his tendency toward secrecy and dictatorial rulings.

There was a strong rumor in the parish that Father O'Herlihy purchased a car for someone who worked in the rectory. He supposedly gave the name of the recipient of the new car as "Sister Pat." By using the title "Sister," it would lead people to believe the car was purchased for an actual religious sister. His own sister's name, the cook in the parish, was Pat. On one occasion, the car dealer was speaking to one of those who leased a car and he reminded that person that Fr. O'Herlihy's sister's lease renewal was coming up.

One day, during Father Dan O'Herlihy's day off, I borrowed my father's pick-up truck, loaded my belongings, and moved out of St. Timothy's. I was fearful that my moving out in O'Herlihy's presence would have resulted in a violent confrontation. I was leaving the parish just as O'Herlihy was returning home from his day off, and we had an unfriendly exchange. I asked him to mail my last payment for saying Masses at St. Timothy's. I never received that payment.

Robert M. Hoatson, Ph.D.

CHAPTER TWENTY-TWO

SEXUAL ABUSE'S HIDDEN ISSUES

While I was still living at Saint Timothy's rectory and while the pastor was increasing his antics to retaliate and harass me, he called me into his room one Sunday afternoon. He had answered a phone call in his room, and it was from the Seaside Beach Police Department.

Seaside Beach is a beautiful seashore community in New Jersey. The police officer asked if Father Dan O'Herlihy knew Andrew Van Houten, and he said yes. The officer told Father O'Herlihy that Andrew was in custody in Seaside Beach for breaking and entering. That past Friday, Andrew had asked me if he could borrow one of the school vans so he could help move some items. I said, "Of course it's okay." I wasn't sure what he was moving, but it was clear that he went to Seaside Beach and was accused of breaking into a house to steal some items. Father Dan O'Herlihy agreed to post his bail, and Andrew was allowed to drive the school van back to northern New Jersey. When he returned, Andrew told Father Dan and me that he entered the house in order to retrieve a watch that had been stolen from him by a group of thugs earlier that evening. Andrew Van Houten tendered his resignation as principal of Our Lady of Good Counsel High School to me that evening.

You might recall in an earlier chapter that I was suspicious of rumors I had heard about Andrew Van Houten when he was a Christian Brother. When he and I were part of a sabbatical program in New York City in 1980, the petty cash box that was meant for the brothers on sabbatical was nearly emptied. One of the Christian Brothers, a classmate of Andrew's, told me that Andrew was rumored to have a problem with taking money from community cash boxes. Since that rumor was never confirmed, I couldn't accuse Andrew of it, but I kept my eye carefully on Our Lady of Good Counsel's money, and Andrew had to have budget items approved by me before he purchased anything major.

After Andrew resigned that Sunday, I phoned the pastor of Our Lady of Good Counsel, Monsignor Plunkett, and told him what had happened. He was shocked, to say the least. I then told the pastor that I was going to ask Harry Hart to become the principal. I called Harry, and he accepted. I thanked him profusely for bailing us out of this mess, and he was thrilled to start school the next day as the principal.

I informed Pat McGrath, the elementary school principal who was a very good friend of Andrew's; Sister Joan Ruth Whittle, another good friend of Andrew's; the Board of Directors of the schools, and the archdiocese. Pat McGrath and Sister Joan Ruth were saddened and disappointed that their friend Andrew would be involved in a law enforcement matter. They just could not believe that something like that could be connected to their dear friend, but they pledged that the schools would not miss a beat, especially with Harry Hart coming on as principal of the high school.

On Monday, I informed the two faculties about what happened and announced that Harry Hart was the new principal of Our Lady of Good Counsel High School. Harry met with the students and told them to go about their academic business and not get caught up in rumors and stories. Only one person expressed doubt about the truth of the story, and I had to speak to her at length.

Sally Rinehart, President of the School Board, did not believe I was telling the whole story. Sally had been appointed to her position by me because she had been a tireless worker on behalf of her alma maters. Her large family mostly attended Our Lady of Good Counsel Schools, and she still lived in the neighborhood in the huge family home. Sally thought I was holding back the truth, but I assured her that I had told her the truth. I told her that the story would probably end up in a newspaper article at the Jersey Shore or beyond, and she could then match my story with the story in the newspaper. Sure enough, the story was featured in a Jersey Shore newspaper and reported as I'd told it to Sally Rinehart.

I knew I told the truth, but I realized later that Sally was "connected" with archdiocesan personnel, especially a religious brother, Brother Raphael Terranova, who was a gossip monger and spread discord throughout the archdiocese. I think Brother Raphael was happy I was embarrassed by what happened, since I was the one who named Andrew Van Houten principal of the high school. Sally turned out to be an antagonist to what we were trying to accomplish. I had to fire her as president of the board.

Brother Raphael Terranova was an interesting character. He was a member of the De La Salle Christian Brothers and a member of the archdiocesan education office for years, rising to the title of Associate Superintendent of Schools. Brother Raphael was two-faced. He would say one thing to one person and a completely different thing to another. I also feared he was a racist and didn't like the appointment of Harry Hart as principal because he was African-American. He made it a point at meetings to say, even publicly, that once the enrollment of a Catholic high school went beyond 50% African-American, the school tended to decline and eventually close. Our Lady of Good Counsel High School's enrollment was primarily African-American and Hispanic. Brother Raphael was not to be trusted. Another elementary school principal sued the Archdiocese of Newark because Brother Raphael claimed that the principal, a male, was picking up men at a county park. It wasn't true, and allegedly the principal received a settlement from the archdiocese.

In addition, as reported to me by the same principal, Brother Raphael was photographed by the same principal patronizing a dirty bookstore in New York City. The bookstore also had stalls for sex. Brother Raphael saw the principal taking pictures of him and chased him down the street. He couldn't catch him, however. I wrote to Brother Raphael's religious and archdiocesan superiors about that event, but nothing was done to discipline him, and he kept his job. That same principal contacted me for assistance when Monsignor Gerald Doherty, an educational leader in the archdiocese, called on him to secure tickets to a Broadway show. The principal happened to be an accomplished musician and had contacts on Broadway. Monsignor Doherty told the principal that if he obtained the tickets for the show, Monsignor Doherty would reserve a room for them at a New York City hotel so they could spend the night together. It was clearly an enticement to use against the principal at a later date if he had accepted.

While I was at Our Lady of Good Counsel Schools, I was also made aware of sexual abuse of a student by a teacher that pre-dated my time there, but the teacher kept his job, too. A Spanish teacher had an affair with a very pretty Hispanic girl. I believe it was Monsignor Joseph Plunkett who made the incident known to me. I phoned the Newark Police Department and Essex County Prosecutor and asked for a complete investigation. I also informed the archdiocesan school's office. I interviewed the young lady, who didn't realize that the teacher's behavior was not only inappropriate, but illegal. She and her family were not happy that I was pursuing the matter, but I explained to her that it was my job to keep her and all students safe from sexual predators. Unfortunately, law enforcement authorities could not pursue the criminal behavior because of New Jersey's statute of limitations at the time. The young lady finished her senior year, graduated, and received a partial scholarship to a major American university.

The tragedy of Andrew Van Houten was especially curious to me, since he had been a fellow Christian Brother for several years and was an enormously talented and popular teacher and administrator. He had been principal of a Catholic high school for a few years and essentially led that school back to financial and academic success. He taught classes while he was principal, something nearly unheard of because of the full-time responsibilities of a full-time principal in this day and age. He was a successful teacher and administrator at an elite prep school, and his stardom was growing in the Christian Brothers. His bizarre interactions with alleged thugs at Seaside Beach did not make sense to me. I wondered if something had interfered in his developing years. Was there something I did not know about Andrew Van Houten? Indeed!

Once Andrew Van Houten's scrape with the Seaside Beach Police ended successfully for all involved, he asked to speak to me about his life. He admitted that he had been sexually abused as a postulant[6] at Columba College by the college chaplain, Father Gerard O'Sullivan. Father O'Sullivan was also pastor of a large parish, not far from Columba College. Andrew was the youngest of the postulants because he graduated high school at the age of 17, so he was considered a child, according to the laws of New York State. He was sexually abused on the Columba College campus by Father O'Sullivan at age 17. The abuse was reported by Andrew to the Archdiocese. Andrew Van Houten was found credible and given a settlement in the Archdiocese Independent Compensation Program. But Andrew's story did not end there.

When Andrew Van Houten was a scholastic and about to finish his college degree at Columba College, he was sent to Bishop Harrington High School in Rhode Island during the winter

---

6 First year member

semester break as a teacher intern. All the scholastics were assigned to different Christian Brothers schools during the break in order to learn more about teaching and learning. They would be housed in extra bedrooms in the various Christian Brothers communities. Bishop Harrington High School was a fairly large school with a substantial residence to house the Christian Brothers.

During Andrew's internship at Bishop Harrington High School, he was introduced to the chaplain of the school, Father Joseph Rocha, OP, a Dominican priest who took care of the sacramental needs of the Christian Brothers community and the student body. Father Rocha lived in the Christian Brothers community, and after a night of drinking, he entered Brother Andrew's room and sexually abused him. From that moment on, Andrew placed a large dresser next to his door so Father Rocha could not enter. This was the second time he had been abused as a member of the Congregation of Christian Brothers. As an adult, Andrew Van Houten filed a claim with Father Rocha's religious order, was found credible, and received a settlement from the religious order. Father Joseph Rocha was removed from Bishop Harrington High School.

Finally, Andrew confided in me that there was one more act of sexual abuse against him, and it was very troublesome and traumatic. In the 1990s, Andrew had taken a leave of absence from the Christian Brothers and was hired as Religious Education Director at Saint Timothy's Parish in Closter, New Jersey. Father Dan O'Herlihy, the pastor, hired him and allowed him to live in the parish rectory. Andrew moved into the rectory and began to supervise a large religious education program for the children of Saint Timothy's Parish. At times, Father Dan O'Herlihy invited him into his suite of rooms to socialize and watch television and movies. According to Andrew, he noticed that Dan O'Herlihy had a stash of pornographic CDs in his room, and at times, when Andrew passed Father Dan's room, he would see Father Dan watching these pornographic movies.

Andrew went into Father Dan's living room and sat in one of his easy chairs. Father Dan poured him a drink, and they began to talk and watch a movie. Soon thereafter, Andrew Van Houten remembered getting sleepy but thought it might be the effects of the alcohol. Andrew must have passed out because he woke up hours later with his clothing missing. He has alleged he was anally raped by Father Dan O'Herlihy. He then left the room and did not know what to do, except try to act as normally in the rectory and with the religious education program as possible. He then confided to me that he reported Father Dan O'Herlihy to the Archdiocese, was found credible, and received a settlement from the Independent Victims' Compensation Program of the Dioceses of New Jersey. I then concluded that Andrew's behavior from the age of 17 until his late 40s was due to his anxieties and traumatic experiences stemming from the sexual abuse he endured. Courageously, Andrew revealed the several acts of abuse that were inflicted upon him and is living a much more stress-free life. He started psychotherapy and has been in therapy ever since. He is recovering beautifully, and I am grateful he said to me, 'I want my story to be told.'

Robert M. Hoatson, Ph.D.

CHAPTER TWENTY-THREE

MY FATHER HAS A STROKE

In 2005, Dr. Geraldine Chapey approached me to say that she could no longer finance the studio apartment in Rockaway Beach because a family member got very sick and needed her financial assistance. I paid for the apartment myself for a little while, but it became too expensive. Then I had an idea. Why don't I sublet the apartment and see if I could eventually earn enough money to go back into it? Through simple word of mouth, the young woman in the local bagel store told me she was looking to rent a place for her and her boyfriend that was close to the store. My building was directly across the street. I asked simply for the rent I was paying month to month, and they moved in. They paid rent on time for the first several months, but then they decided to move to Delaware, so they didn't bother paying rent for the last couple of months. I had to pay for one month myself, and the building management kept my security deposit as the last month's rent.

It was time for me to move anyway, because my parents needed my help at home. My father had suffered a severely debilitating stroke in 1996, and my mother had taken care of him by herself for ten years. My father could not bathe himself, feed himself, or walk without assistance, so my mother's job was full time and more. When I asked my parents if it would be helpful for me to move in with them, they jumped at the suggestion.

Living with my parents was ideal for all three of us. By that time, my father was 81 years old and my mother was 79. I was 51 years old and in relatively excellent health (not even the C1Q Nephropathy disease had any symptoms). Since my father needed to be in a separate room and bed than my mother because of his ailments, I reclaimed what was known as the back bedroom, which was close to my father, so I could hear him and get up in the middle of the night if necessary.

I set up the Road to Recovery, Inc. office in what had been my sister's room, just large enough for a decent sized office. The arrangement was perfect.

CHAPTER TWENTY-FOUR

FRONT PAGE NEWS

In 2006, after I filed my RICO lawsuit, I was contacted by a reporter for a popular New York newspaper, especially in the gay community, the *Village Voice*. Kristen Lombardi had worked for the *Boston Phoenix* and was the first journalist in America to expose the Catholic Church's clergy abuse cover-up. Kristen met me in a Starbucks in the East Village of Manhattan, and we talked for hours. Her photographer then met me in front of the Cathedral Basilica of the Sacred Heart in Newark for a photo shoot. Never did I imagine that I would be on the front page of the *Village Voice* with a headline that read, "Outing Cardinal Egan." The information I gave Kristen came from Carol Stanford, a Catholic, New York, elementary school principal who blew the whistle on her pastor for frequenting gay bars and keeping a male prostitute in the parish rectory. She lost her job as a result, but Carol had another secret she wanted to tell.

A relative of hers, a religious brother, was rumored to be the boyfriend of Cardinal Edward Egan, of the New York Archdiocese from 2000–2009. Before he was assigned to the New York Archdiocese, Egan was the bishop of Bridgeport, Connecticut, from 1988–2000. It was when Carol's relative was principal of a Connecticut Catholic high school that he and then-Bishop Egan met. They became "special friends," according to Carol Stanford, and when that religious brother went to Rome, Cardinal Egan made sure he stayed in Vatican City in first-class accommodations. Carol told me that she had her relative on audio tape talking about the "special friendship" he had with Cardinal Egan, and that she would give it to the media or me. I told Kristen Lombardi about that, but Carol got cold feet and did not turn over the tape. However, she did say that Cardinal Egan and her brother traveled together, and

Cardinal Egan even attended Stanford family wakes and funerals, including that of Carol's religious brother relative who died at a young age.

 The religious brother relative of Carol's had become the president of his order, but then developed a cancer that spread rather quickly throughout his body. He spent his final days in the infirmary of a religious community of women, of which one of his sisters was a member. Unfortunately, some religious men who die at a young age of cancer are, in reality, often victims of another disease; namely, AIDS. I am not claiming in any way that her relative died of AIDS, but it has been a policy of religious orders to use the code word "cancer" to describe AIDS deaths.

 After four years living with my parents, my father died on March 3, 2010 at the age of 85, two days before my parents' 61st wedding anniversary. He lived for fourteen years with the effects of a stroke. He was a veteran of the Marine Corps and fought in the Pacific region during World War II. He came from a Scottish Presbyterian family. His mother was from Paisley, and his father was born in Glasgow. I didn't know my grandfather well, since he died in 1957 when I was just five years old. He had been a successful carpenter and built many expensive homes and mansions locally. Unfortunately, he lost everything in The Great Depression. My grandmother I knew well, since she lived until the age of 99 and eleven months. Since I was in religious life at the time, I conducted her funeral in 1989 at a local Protestant church. I loved her Scottish burr, but have never been able to imitate it, and the entire family loved her baked goods, such as Scottish shortbread. At times, I would play some of her favorite Protestant hymns on the piano or organ, and we would sing together.

After my father died, I had more time to go on the road to help victims. My mother was in fairly good health, and she didn't mind me leaving her alone while I traveled to Boston; upstate New York; Florida; Ohio; Chicago; Detroit; Altoona and Johnstown, Pennsylvania; London, UK; Dublin, Ireland; and many other cities, states, and countries, including Ghana. At first, she was not supportive of my work, but then she realized how serious the clergy sexual abuse crisis was. She was hesitant to criticize her church, but she was beginning to see the light. I was increasing my media events, appearing on Court TV with Nancy Grace, who called me a hero priest for blowing the whistle on the cover-up by the Church. I also went on Anderson Cooper's show a couple of times on CNN to speak about the Church's scandal. I was a regular on local New Jersey and New York media, including the *New York Times*, *Newark Star Ledger*, and New York television stations such as WABC, WNBC, WPIX, and WCBS. News 12 New Jersey also interviewed me often.

However, about a year before my father passed, I had to deal with one of the most traumatic events of my life. I started getting repressed memories returning to my consciousness. Dr. William Richardson was my psychiatrist at the time, and I had been working with him for about ten years when I started experiencing repressed memories. They usually returned just as I was waking up in the morning, and they scared me to death.

Robert M. Hoatson, Ph.D.

CHAPTER TWENTY-FIVE

REPRESSED MEMORY COMES FLOODING BACK

Keep in mind that Dr. Richardson was my therapist for twenty years, and before Dr. Richardson, Dr. Ronald Sorvino was my psychiatrist. I first went to see Dr. Sorvino in approximately 1983 when I was 31 years old after my brother and sister-in-law intervened in my life; they could clearly see that I was not in good shape psychologically. They sat me down in their house and got right to the point. They asked, "What is going on with you, Bobby?" Their concern impressed me, and I told them about Brother Martin Francis Connelly sexually abusing me from 1979 until 1982, and the damage he and others had done was written all over my face. I also told them the story of the sexual abuse by Brother Giordano and Brother Matthew Aquinas. They were most sympathetic and outraged.

My brother and sister-in-law told me about a psychiatrist by the name of Dr. Ronald Sorvino. He was Paul Sorvino the actor's brother and the uncle of actress Mia Sorvino. He practiced in the town of New Providence and worked out of Overlook Hospital in Summit, New Jersey. He saw me once or twice when I was home visiting my family, but I was still stationed in Boston, so he got me started on the right road and promised me he would continue as my therapist when I returned to New York or New Jersey. He said it would be good if I could get into therapy while stationed in Boston. I agreed to find a competent therapist.

When I returned to Boston, I began to research therapists. There was an organization called the The House of Affirmation that was founded in central Massachusetts. A nun and a priest founded the mental health services for priests, deacons, nuns, and religious brothers. The House of Affirmation had an inpatient facility at its headquarters and a few outpatient facilities throughout the country, including the city of Boston.

I contacted the outpatient office in downtown Boston, and I was accepted into the program. Father J.A. Loftus, S.J. became my therapist, and he was terrific. I not only saw Father Loftus once a week, but I got involved in a group therapy workshop at their site in the Fenway section of Boston. For nearly three years, I attended therapy sessions at The House of Affirmation and took medicine that was prescribed by my psychiatrist, Dr. Robert Arnot, and the staff psychiatrist there. I came to understand how much I needed therapy to process the extensive sexual abuse I experienced.

In 1985, I was notified by Fordham University that I was being offered a graduate assistantship to finish my Ph.D. in educational administration and church leadership. The year before, Fordham University offered me a full scholarship to complete my degree, but the provincial of the Christian Brothers asked me to turn it down and remain at Catholic Memorial High School for another year. I was somewhat disappointed, but I loved working with the students of Catholic Memorial High School, so I considered my final year there a bonus.

I hesitatingly left Boston in June, 1985, and moved to New York City. It was not an easy transfer, since I received a letter from Christian Brothers headquarters that I would be living at All Hallows High School located in the shadow of Yankee Stadium in the Bronx. I am not sure if I was more disappointed or furious that I had been assigned to a Christian Brothers community in the Bronx that was nowhere near where I would be studying at Fordham University near Lincoln Center in Manhattan. The graduate school of education was located on the Manhattan campus, a short walk from the Christian Brothers community on West 51st Street and Ninth Avenue.

I contacted headquarters and reminded the "bosses" that the West Side Community would be much more convenient (and less expensive) to my studies at the Fordham University campus in Manhattan. I asked to be assigned to Christian Brothers West Side, a five-story brownstone housing approximately six or seven Christian Brothers. There was plenty of room there for me, so the provincial council changed my assignment to that community. I wondered why they had assigned me to the Bronx in the first place. The answer was infuriating.

Soon after I moved into a fifth-floor bedroom at Christian Brothers West Side, I learned that the members of that community voted not to allow me to move in, so the provincial council assigned me to the Bronx community. It turns out that I was not welcome because most of the "West Siders" were leading secret lives, and they were afraid that I would object to brothers who were dating their secretaries, having sex with fellow teachers, and getting involved in the leadership of an unauthorized gay Catholic organization. One brother, the principal of a Catholic elementary school in lower Manhattan, moved a young boy into our house without explanation, and a woman named Gladys rang our doorbell frequently to complain about the brother. I am not sure if that Christian Brother was involved with that woman, or if the child living in our community was her son, but the situation was less than appropriate. That Christian Brother, who eventually married, was a national education leader in the Catholic Church.

I lived at Christian Brothers West Side for nearly six years, finishing my Ph.D. in 1987. My doctoral committee was made up of three professors; including two Jesuits and a female professor.

Robert M. Hoatson, Ph.D.

CHAPTER TWENTY-SIX

ANXIETY SETS IN, I SEEK HELP

From the time I moved from Boston to New York in 1985, I was treated by Dr. A. Ronald Sorvino. It was becoming more and more uncommon for a psychiatrist to conduct psychotherapy as well as psychopharmacology, but Dr. Sorvino did both. I saw him for forty-five-minute sessions once a week for a year or more, and then he asked me to join a therapy group that he led in the evenings. Dr. Sorvino helped me realize that I was preyed upon by a number of persons in my life, and he advised me to stay away from all of the people who groomed and sexually abused me. In 1996, Dr. Sorvino retired and recommended that I switch to one of his partners, Dr. William T. Richardson, another psychiatrist who conducted psychotherapy sessions. However, I decided to "wing it" and not engage in therapy any longer. By that time, I was living in the seminary and preparing for ordination to the priesthood. I remember having an anxiety attack after being told that I would not be ordained to the priesthood that year. Archbishop McCarrick did not call me to Holy Orders, and I was heartbroken. It was my impression when I first met with him in 1994 that I would be a seminarian for about two years and then be ordained. 1994–1996 represented two years, so I set myself up for ordination.

I had a serious anxiety attack the night I was passed over for ordination and made an appointment with Dr. Sorvino. Even though he retired, he was still treating some of his long-term clients on a part-time basis, so he agreed to see me on an emergency basis. He calmed me down by asking me when my ordination would most likely take place. I told him I probably would be ordained a priest in 1997. He told me that was not something to worry about and that I should remain in the seminary and wait until 1997. I did what he advised and didn't obsess on the fact that I was not called to ordination in 1996. I was, however, called to the diaconate in 1996, which meant priestly ordination would take place a year later.

I remained relatively anxiety-free during my diaconate year, which took place at Saint Margaret of Cortona Parish in Little Ferry, NJ. I mentioned earlier that the pastor was not very welcoming, but I got through the year in relative happiness. I really enjoyed preaching and visiting the sick, but I could not wait until May 24, 1997, the day my class was scheduled to be ordained. How did I know the date? Because priestly ordinations in the Newark Archdiocese take place on Memorial Day weekend every year. Of course, with a transfer in 1996 to a parish and then anticipating priestly ordination in 1997, my anxiety was high, but my excitement was higher. I continued to "wing it" psychologically throughout 1996 and 1997. Things would change drastically in 1998.

In 1998, I was assigned to Holy Trinity Parish in Hackensack, New Jersey, the city seat of Bergen County. Recall that I had asked for a transfer because of the lack of compassion and sympathy for a family whose two sons were sexually abused by a priest at St. Luke's in Hudson County. At Holy Trinity, I was stationed with a bishop, Sean Scanlon, who was a one-star general in the Army chaplaincy and the pastor; an administrator of the parish, Father Ben Ippolito, who was once a Christian Brother with me and whom I knew fairly well; a Colombian priest who took care of the Latino population; and a deacon assigned to the parish who was preparing for priestly ordination. Recall, too, that two of those priests, the bishop and the administrator, verbally assaulted me one morning as I ate breakfast in the rectory kitchen. It turned out that Father Ben Ippolito, the parish administrator, had left me a message very late one evening, just as I was leaving for my day off. I ignored the message because I did not have the time to respond or consider his request. I had made plans to meet people shortly after my day off was to begin.

The bishop and the administrator walked in together, and the bishop started screaming, "Where were you yesterday? Do you know that there was no one on duty?" I responded, "I was on my day off." The administrator then said, "I left you a note to handle duty for me yesterday." I responded, "I know you did, but I never told you I could do it, so you should have stayed for duty or asked someone else to take duty." The bishop kept screaming some nonsense, but I didn't hear much because I tuned him out.

However, I went to my room, closed the door, and had a massive anxiety attack. I took some medicine that I had left over (Paxil, I think) and some Valium, and I waited for the medicine to kick in. I left my room to say Mass and fulfill my obligations as a priest, but nothing else. I wanted to pack my bags and leave that rectory for good.

Instead, I remembered that Dr. Ronald Sorvino had recommended that I continue in therapy with Dr. William Richardson, so I phoned his office and made an appointment. On October 1, 1998 (my brother Bill's birthday), I had my first session with Dr. Richardson. I thought the world of Dr. Sorvino and hoped that Dr. Richardson would be as good. I was pleasantly surprised. Dr. Richardson was better, and I spent the next 20 years with him. Dr. Richardson advised that I take some medicine (Lexapro) because I was depressed and Valium because I was anxious. I told him about what happened at the rectory, and he asked me what I was feeling at the moment. I told him I wanted nothing to do with the bishop or the administrator, and he said, "Then don't have anything to do with them." I explained that I had to eat dinner with them each night, and he said, "Why? Are you by contract required to eat with the bishop or the administrator?" I answered, "No, I am not."

I felt myself getting more and more assertive. I then said, "I will have nothing to do with them outside my official priestly duties." "That's a plan," Dr. Richardson said, "and let's see each other in a week." Dr. Richardson turned out to be one of the most ethical, moral, and professional doctors I have ever met. He was honored late in his career by the *New York Times*, which placed him in the centerfold of their newspaper as the "Finest Psychiatrist in the United States." He retired on July 31, 1998, and I cried my eyes out. His receptionist, Gloria, and I cried together before I left his office. He was simply the greatest!

Dr. Richardson recommended that I start with a therapist who was in his practice, but I wanted to think about it. I was having trouble paying for expensive therapy since my medical benefits with the Archdiocese of Newark ended in 2010. I thought I needed to find a therapist who took Medicare. I did research and found a therapist who took Medicare, so I called her and made an appointment. It was the fall of 1998, and I had not been in therapy since July 31. Dr. Anne did an intake with me, and she agreed to become my therapist. She spent most of the first session getting biographical and financial information. The second session was approximately a week later, and that would be the last. I had told her some details about a repressed memory regarding sexual abuse, and she told me that a repressed memory is not a universally accepted event. She then tried to convince me that the person who abused me really did not abuse me. I had a serious anxiety attack as I left her office and in bed that night. We were scheduled to meet the next week. For one week, I agonized over whether I would return or not.

The day of the next appointment, I phoned her and said, "Dr. Anne, I will not be coming this afternoon for therapy. I did not agree with your opinion about repressed memory or the analysis of the abuse I described. I just finished with a psychiatrist in July with whom I was making great strides with repressed memories. Thank you, but I will not be coming back." As soon as I made the decision not to return to Dr. Anne, I felt one hundred percent better. I began to research therapists once again, but God had other plans for me. I phoned a few therapists but for one reason or another, not one of them was available. That was a Friday, and my car's oil was due to be changed the next day.

I arrived at S&R Automotive on Saturday morning at around 7:40 a.m. I tried to arrive early because Bob Rourke's weekend mechanic, Steve, was always available early. He saw me coming and opened up the bay door, directing me onto the mechanical lift. I often waited for my car to be serviced, paid my bill, and went on my way. Bob Rourke was my parents' mechanic for over thirty years, and I remained with him because of his expertise and honesty. He is a talented mechanic who explains and shows you what he does to your car. In addition, his shop is like a clubhouse for many of the old-timers and some young guys who enjoy Bob's company and love his work.

While I was sitting on one of Bob's overused recliners, a gentleman walked into the shop. Bob humorously yelled out to me, "Bob, be careful, here comes the shrink. He might psychoanalyze you." He introduced him to me and me to him. "Bob, this is Ben; Ben this is Bob. Ben, Bob is a former priest, so watch your language." Ben bantered back and forth with Bob Rourke and finally said that he was there for a tire change or some other repair. Bob then told me that Ben was a psychotherapist who often volunteered at the Veterans Hospital in East Orange, New Jersey, to help the men and women with post-traumatic stress disorder. As soon as he said that, my ears perked up, and I said to myself, *I wonder if he is taking on clients?* I left after my car was serviced and decided to google Ben's name. Bob Rourke mentioned his last name, but it was a long, Italian name with "vicar" at the beginning. I knew the term "vicar" because it means "priest" in Italian. I found a Ben Vicarisi online whose office was located near my residence. I waited until Monday and phoned his number.

I said, "Mr. Vicarisi, this is Bob. We met at Bob Rourke's shop last Saturday. I am wondering if you are accepting new clients." He responded, "Sure, why don't you come in, and we can talk." His office was a five-minute drive from my apartment building, and I went in for my first appointment. It went beautifully. Ben thought he might be able to help me, and I thought I could talk to him openly and honestly. As I left, I asked him, "How much do I owe you?" He said, "Don't worry about it, we'll talk about that once we get into it." Ben Vicarisi has been my therapist ever since, and I believe it was God who brought us together. Ben is a Catholic who once worked for Catholic Charities and Health and Hospitals. I once worked for Catholic Charities and Health and Hospitals, too, and I think Ben and I may have met before, but we couldn't pinpoint where or when. We knew many of the same people.

My sessions with Ben Vicarisi have been extraordinarily helpful. He has helped me continue my processing of repressed memories and believe in myself that I am telling the truth. After all, I said to him, "Who could or would want to make this up?" I would trade everything and anything I own not to have lived with the effects of sexual abuse almost my entire life. My headaches, gastrointestinal issues, surprise diseases, and psychological distresses are not figments of my imagination. They are all interconnected with the aftermath of childhood sexual abuse. I have come a long way toward recovery but will have challenges the rest of my life. I am committed to doing whatever it takes to live as healthy a life as possible.

CHAPTER TWENTY-SEVEN

OFFICE POLITICS

After the oral defense of my doctoral dissertation in October, 1987, Dr. Bertha Livingston, a former professor of mine and president of a large publishing company, Jacob Hartstein and Sons, and a nationally recognized educational expert, asked me to join her as assistant to the president of the company. She had heard about the fiasco surrounding the rescinding of the offer I had received from Dr. Jerry Starratt to run the Fordham Center for Non-Public Education, which seemed final. However, the Dean of the School of Education, Dr. Max Weiner, had other plans. He appointed one of his graduate assistants, an Australian nun, to that position. I was furious but had no recourse. I told Dr. Livingston I would seriously consider her offer. Brother Felix O'Shaughnessy, yes *that* Brother Felix O'Shaughnessy, the one who told me I was a cold person years earlier, had been elected provincial and gave me permission to work at the publishing company, so I accepted Dr. Livingston's offer.

I thought the Christian Brothers would have had some idea how best to use my talents and Ph.D., but there was no such luck. The Christian Brothers is primarily an educational religious order, so it seemed automatic to me that I would be tapped to do something in educational administration since that was the basis of my Ph.D. After I had accepted the position with the publishing company and gotten my feet wet in that business, the Christian Brothers West Side community had its annual provincial visitation. The provincial councilperson chosen to conduct the visitation was Brother Louis William D'Andrea.

Brother D'Andrea asked me, "Bob, what would be a good time for us to talk?" I responded, "Lou, we will have to talk tomorrow because I am leaving later in the day tomorrow on a week-long caravan for the publishing company giving talks and workshops on catechetics (religious education)." He said, "Fine, suppose we meet in the front parlor in the morning some time." I responded, "I will meet you there with my suitcase ready to go." Brother Lou and I met, and his first question was "Bob, now that you have finished your doctoral degree, what do think you want to do?" "I would like to be a secondary school principal," I responded. Without batting an eye, Brother Lou looked at me and said, "Oh, Bob, as long as I am on the provincial council, you will never be a secondary school principal because I am reserving those positions for people I like."

Since I had been used to the political machinations in the religious life from the time I entered, I didn't respond to Brother Lou. I was angry, of course, and wanted to shake him into reality. Instead, I excused myself, telling him I had to get going to the airport. I picked up my suitcase and left. When I returned from the trip, I confided in my community superior, Brother John Roche, what Brother Lou had said, and he was as shocked as I was. We then began to name the Christian Brothers whom Brother Lou favored.

Fortunately, I had a job working at a publishing company and worked with some of the finest people I had ever met. I helped write religion textbooks, parent manuals, and actually co-wrote a religious education program for the Archdiocese of Los Angeles.

Once I moved back to New York in 1985, I got into full-time psychotherapy with Dr. Ronald Sorvino. Because I was working with the publishing company, I had to purchase a car, so I bought a Toyota Corolla and parked in a local garage for free. We had a connection with a local politician, who arranged the free parking spot. Dr. Sorvino saw me one-on-one once a week and asked me to join a group therapy session one other day a week in the evening. In addition, he asked me to stay for what he called "alternate group therapy," which was an hour-and-a-half session after group therapy with just the members of the group present. We sat in his waiting room and ran the meeting ourselves, continuing the facilitated group session that just ended.

Unfortunately, my employment with the publishing company was not working out well. Dr. Bertha Livingston, whom I adored as my professor and mentor at Fordham University, was not the same person as president of the publishing company. I took as many courses as I could with Dr. Livingston because she was a brilliant teacher and scholar, but her role as a company CEO was nothing short of bizarre. I was the assistant to the president, and she told some of the executive team that I probably would succeed her as president, but I had other plans because of her inconsistent behavior. My cubicle was located on the executive floor, but I had little to nothing to do. When Dr. Livingston wanted to see me, she threw open her office door and screamed, "Bob Hoatson, get in here now." She did it with a number of people, including the owners of the company.

The company, which had been in the family for decades, was one of the most profitable book companies in the country. The company published vocabulary books, math books, and religion books, to name a few. When they hired Dr. Bertha Livingston, it was because she was very well respected in the Catholic and public education communities, nationally and internationally, and could guarantee the selling of books galore, but her role as a company CEO was, in my opinion, troublesome. The lay people who worked there were sweethearts, and I made life-long friendships, but I could not take Dr. Bertha Livingston's inconsistent behavior. Fear permeated the company while she was president. I knew I had to get out, so I began sending my resumé to various educational institutions. Since I wasn't going to get a job in the Christian Brothers' schools, I focused on other schools.

One of the institutions I contacted was St. John's University School of Education and Human Services in New York City. To my amazement, I received a phone call from Dr. Geraldine Chapey, who set up a time for an interview. The position was Assistant Dean of the School of Education in charge of undergraduate education. It sounded perfect. Dr. Chapey informed me that the position was formerly hers and that she was promoted to Dean of the School of Education and Human Services. Geraldine Chapey was a 70-something-year-old, New York City Board of Education retiree whose energy was that of a thirty-year old. My interview lasted about four hours because she kept getting up to help students at the counter. It was impressive how she dealt with late teens and twenty-year olds. She offered me the job, and I accepted.

I gave Dr. Bertha Livingston my two-week notice, and she immediately turned on me. The next day, I was scheduled to go to Covington, Kentucky, to give talks and workshops to educators about the company's textbooks, but Dr. Livingston called me into her office and said, "Bob, you can leave now. Please clean out your desk." At least she didn't have someone escort me out like she had done to two other women, former nuns, who left for the same reasons I left. The three of us often commiserated about Bertha's arrogant and mean-spirited demeanor, and we knew our days were numbered. Both women were as moral and ethical as can be, but Dr. Livingston had both of them escorted out of the Park Place, Manhattan, building. It was insulting and demeaning. I think I escaped that fate because I was an executive of the company, and it would have gotten around the building that Brother Hoatson, Livingston's heir apparent, was escorted out of the fourth floor by one of the company executives.

Dr. Geraldine Chapey could not have been a better supervisor as Dean of the School of Education and Human Services at St. John's University. She allowed my creative side to flourish as I decorated our offices and hallway as an elementary, middle, or high school would be decorated. I tried to motivate the education majors to love students, schools, and education in general. One of the major changes I made was to make the semester registration process more humane. I asked the undergraduate faculty to occupy our large main office and make themselves available to help students choose courses. We offered refreshments while discussion groups offered suggestions to improve coursework, student teaching, and scheduling of courses that was more realistic. There were approximately 700 undergraduate education majors, and most were preparing to enter New York City and Long Island public schools. We also had close relations with the Catholic school systems of the Archdiocese of New York, and the Dioceses of Brooklyn and Rockville Centre, Long Island.

My year at St. John's University was proceeding beautifully, except for my interaction with the university's president, Father Joseph Cahill. I saw Father Cahill one lunchtime in Marillac Hall, where the School of Education and Human Services was located. The cafeteria in Marillac Hall was famous for its pizza slices. One would never expect a university cafeteria to have gourmet food, but the pizza was the best I ever had, including to this day. I approached Father Cahill and introduced myself. "Hello, Father Cahill, my name is Brother Bob Hoatson, the new assistant dean in the School of Education and Human Services." His response, or lack thereof, shocked me. He merely grunted, "Huh," and walked away. I never saw him again. I thought to myself as I carried my slice of pizza back to my office, *Another whack job*. When I told the dean about my experience with Father Cahill, she was not surprised, and Father Cahill's behavior would turn even more bizarre as the year went on.

Father Cahill, a priest from a religious order, had been president of St. John's University for twenty-four years and was looking forward to celebrating his twenty-fifth anniversary as president. His sycophantic followers were excited about throwing him a big bash. However, Cahill's superiors had other plans. The provincial of the religious order, believe it or not, had greater authority than Father Cahill and could assign him to any ministry he wanted. He informed Cahill that he would not be renewed as president after

1989. Cahill was outraged and began calculating a way to remain president.

Father Cahill called all the deans of the various schools together for a meeting and demanded that each of them wear a green armband to protest the actions of the provincial and demand that Father Donald J. Harrington's appointment as the new president be rescinded. St. John's had several schools, such as Arts and Sciences, Pharmacy, Education, Law, Chinese Studies, and many others, and every dean wore the green armband, except one. Dr. Geraldine Chapey refused to wear the armband because she thought it was a stunt by Father Cahill to gain popularity. She resented being used as a ploy to save Cahill's position. As a result, Father Cahill called Dr. Chapey in and told her that she was being replaced as Dean of the School of Education and Human Services by a professor in the School of Education and Human Services who was unable to teach even the basic course in administration and asked me to teach it. The new dean cemented his spot in the university by picking up and driving a previous university administrator to school every day for several years.

I had little to no respect for the new dean because he was dishonest and deceptive. He smiled at you while placing the knife in your back. Dr. Chapey was a refreshing professional as dean, and her connections with educational leaders throughout New York State and beyond were impressive. Before she died at 98 years old, she served as a member of the prestigious Board of Regents of the state of New York for many years. By avocation, she was a speech pathologist but quickly became a New York City high school principal and program director. At one time, she ran the Board of Education's Title I program for Catholic schools. She rued the day that she was demoted from a job she had just been named to a few months before, and she feared for the School of Education and Human Services with the new so-called leader because she felt the school would suffer severely.

Father Joseph Cahill did not fire Dr. Geraldine Chapey from her professorship, only her deanship, but she was embarrassed and humiliated. She confided in me that she never thought a priest in her church would be so arrogant and corrupt. One of her daughters had graduated from St. John's, and Dr. Chapey had developed several friendships with priests with whom she worked on the Staten Island and Jamaica campuses. Basically, she was in shock, as were most of the professors in the School of Education and Human Services. I contemplated my next move.

I convinced Dr. Chapey to make an appointment with Father Joseph Murphy, the provincial of the order, whose office was in Philadelphia, to plead her case. More than likely, Father Murphy would not have been aware of the antics of Father Joseph Cahill relative to the deans of the schools. She phoned Father Murphy, and he agreed to meet with Dr. Chapey and me. A courageous undergraduate professor of education, Virginia Cavanaugh, who had taught at St. John's for several decades, asked to accompany us to the meeting, so the three of us made our way to Pennsylvania to meet with Father Joseph Murphy.

Father Joseph Murphy seemed to be sympathetic to the pleas of Dr. Chapey to be reinstated as dean, and he promised to speak to Father Donald J. Harrington, the newly appointed president, about what Father Cahill did to Dr. Chapey and ask him to act. We returned to St. John's with a glimmer of hope, but my experience with religious orders and priests told me that nothing would happen, so I gave the newly-named dean my two-week notice of resignation. I could not remain at St. John's because of the way Dr. Chapey was treated and because of the new so-called leader of the School of Education and Human Services. Since it was May already, I had to hustle to find employment, especially if I wanted to be a school administrator.

Robert M. Hoatson, Ph.D.

CHAPTER TWENTY-EIGHT

EDUCATOR OF THE YEAR

I phoned Sister Martha De Santis, Associate Superintendent of Schools for the Archdiocese of New York, and asked her if there were any openings for principals of high schools in the archdiocese. She responded, "It is quite late, Bob, and most schools have filled those positions. However, Sacred Heart High School in Yonkers is looking for a principal, but I think the search committee may have chosen someone to fill that slot. I would recommend calling the pastor immediately to see if their search is still in progress." I thanked her, hung up, and dialed Sacred Heart Parish, asking to speak to Father Philip Fabiano, pastor and a Capuchin priest.

Father Philip Fabiano was very cordial on the telephone, and he mentioned that the search committee had essentially finished its work. They had supposedly settled on a religious sister to become principal. However, he said to me, "What are your qualifications?" I mentioned that I was a Christian Brother, had a doctoral degree in education, and was leaving St. John's University as assistant dean of the School of Education and Human Services. He then said, "Okay, why don't you come in for an interview? I will alert the search committee that we will have one more interview." I expressed my deep thanks to Father Philip Fabiano and began preparing for my interview.

Commencement that year at Sacred Heart High School was Friday, June 3, 1989. I was interviewed early that week and chosen as principal the day before graduation ceremonies in the parish church. Father Philip Fabiano suggested that I attend the graduation and sit in the back of the church to get an idea of what the school was like. Sacred Heart High School was a co-educational, parish high school located on the top of one of the many hilltops in Yonkers, also known as Little San Francisco because of its numerous hills. I took over as principal in June, 1989, and remained there until June, 1994, when I entered the seminary to become a priest. Father Philip Fabiano and I became best of friends, and his outstanding priestly example moved me to leave the Christian Brothers and become a priest.

After two years as principal of Sacred Heart High School, Father Philip Fabiano asked me to consider taking on added responsibilities as director of Total Parish Education. He met me in my office and asked, "Would you consider being in charge of the high school, elementary school, and religious education program?" He was impressed with some of the academic changes I had made in the high school, like Block Scheduling, and an interdisciplinary project for sophomores that some faculty members collaborated in, that attempted to help students see the connections between subjects. Our block scheduling lengthened periods to eighty minutes to enable students and teachers to really delve into subject matter and allowed students to take 3-4 subjects each day instead of the usual 6-7 subjects. The Associate Principal for Academics, a life-long parishioner of Sacred Heart Parish and a graduate of both its schools, Mrs. Helen Nevin, one of the finest educators and persons I have ever met and worked with, was a scheduling genius and worked with myself and the faculty to be more creative academically. These changes led to my being named Educator of the Year in 1990 by the Association of Teachers of New York City.

One of the most daunting challenges I faced as Director of Total Parish Education was convincing the three entities that we were "one" educational component and our students in all three programs were part of one academic enterprise. The parish had two school buildings, an elementary school and a high school. The high school building was a mammoth structure with two main sections: an older, original high school that housed a smaller school connected by a breezeway, to a more modern school in the round which was four stories high. A previous pastor, Father

Finian Sullivan, was famous for "going big" and he was responsible for the round building and two more senior citizen buildings a few blocks from the parish.

Another significant challenge I had as director of schools was beginning to convince the faculties, staffs, parish council, and parents that there was plenty of room in the high school building to house both schools. The original elementary school building was across the street from the high school and the church, and did not contain a cafeteria. Every school day, the elementary school children had to don sweaters, jackets, and other apparel to cross the street, proceed down a steep hill that was a parking lot for the faculty, staff, and students, and enter the high school cafeteria for lunch. It made sense for the elementary school to move across the street to the high school building in order to avoid unnecessary movement for smaller children.

Needless to say, the proposal to move the elementary school from its original location to the high school building created significant pushback and complaints, primarily from the elementary school parents. At a contentious meeting of the parish council, Father Philip Fabiano and I were taken over the coals by the parents suggesting that their elementary-aged children would be exposed to "those big bad high school students." After all, some of them smoked and cursed and acted out, as if there were no elementary school students who did the same thing in imitation of their parents. Father Philip Fabiano and I then revealed a reality that was not clear to the parish council or the parents; namely, that Catholic education was in crisis and schools were closing at a dramatic rate. We had to deliver the news that if we did not do something creative and forward-looking, our two schools may not exist in ten years. Tuitions were rising substantially in order to pay for schools, and that trend was eliminating the families for whom Catholic education was founded: poor and working-class families.

Robert M. Hoatson, Ph.D.

The Assistant Superintendent of Westchester Catholic Schools of the Archdiocese of New York, a deacon, also tried to sabotage Father Philip and me, but he was removed from his position shortly thereafter for allegations of sexual abuse.

It was then that Father Philip Fabiano and I revealed what we had been researching for a couple of years. There was a private school in Westchester County that was interested in renting our elementary school building. The school was for children who were experiencing special needs, and the building was perfect for the mission of the school. In addition, the rent the parish would accrue from the rental would be approximately $300,000 per year. That rental money, we explained, would more than adequately help pay for the subsidy needed to keep our two schools flourishing. Our proposal was still not comforting for many parents, and some contacted the archdiocesan schools' office and Father Philip Fabiano's superiors, requesting that Father Philip Fabiano and I be replaced.

When cooler heads prevailed, the parish council approved the move of the elementary school to the high school building, and the elementary school had better and more convenient facilities and classrooms than it did in the older building across the street. In addition, the high school students loved having the younger kids around, treating them like little brothers and sisters, and the elementary school children felt like "big boys and girls" being among the bigger kids. The entire bottom floor of the building emptied out onto the rear parking lot, and restrooms once reserved for the high school students were reserved for the elementary school. With few minor exceptions, the elementary children were much happier in the high school building. In addition, Sacred Heart Parish began collecting over $30,000 per month for the rental of the former elementary school building. I am pleased to announce that both schools continue to flourish a quarter of a century after the realignment, and the rent continues to be collected. Imagine what the rental fee is today if it was just over $300,000 in 1993–1994.

Father Philip Fabiano completed his six-year term in 1993 but asked his superior for another year in order to complete the realignment process and continue to "calm the troops" after two years of dissent, unfair treatment and insults, and outright lying about the change in educational opportunities at Sacred Heart Church and Schools.

I believe the superior of Father Philip Fabiano, a classmate of his, was jealous of him, refused Father Philip Fabiano's request and removed him as pastor, replacing him with another member of the religious order, a nice enough man who did not work well with me or the accomplishments of his predecessor. I decided that 1993–1994 would be my last year at Sacred Heart Church and Schools because I thought that the new pastor would eventually prefer to have a different leader at the helm.

I announced that I would be leaving at the end of the 1993–1994 school year to enter the seminary of the Archdiocese of Newark to become a priest. It was Father Philip Fabiano's holiness, administrative skills, and priesthood that convinced me I should follow a dream I had as a young boy of becoming a priest.

It was in the seventh and eighth grades, and my friend Joseph Kenneally and I went to Mass every day during Lent. The nuns allowed us to bring our breakfast to school so we could abide by the three-hour fast regulation that was in place at the time. After Mass, Joe and I would go back to class, open our breakfasts at our desks, and get nourishment for the day. It was after a Lenten Mass in the eighth grade when Monsignor Robert Fitzsimmons, our arthritic, severely stooped-over, older pastor, placed the Blessed Sacrament back in the tabernacle following Benediction that I heard the voice of God in my head that said, *Bob, someday you will be a priest.* I was surprised and excited to hear that message as I knelt in the back of the church with Joe kneeling next to me, but I never forgot it. I also believe Joe Kenneally would have been a terrific priest as well.

Robert M. Hoatson, Ph.D.

CHAPTER TWENTY-NINE

EVEN IN ELEMENTARY SCHOOL

Joseph Kenneally actually was my closest friend in elementary school. He was an outstanding student, person, and athlete and came from a great family. The Kenneally family lived a few short blocks from the parish, and Joe walked home after school. He had a brother and sister who went through the parish school, too, and the highlight of our friendship was the lunchtime basketball games we had in the school yard. Joe and another good basketball player, Tommy Benson, were best of friends, too, and they organized equally balanced teams that resulted in fabulously close and competitive games. We were usually very sweaty returning to class after recess, but we sure released whatever was stressing us out.

Tommy Benson became a golf professional after high school and competed in tournaments throughout the east coast. The third member of our leadership team was Timmy Egan, a tiny kid who could play basketball very competitively, even among the kids who were much taller. Unfortunately, Timmy died at a young age. Angelo Di Pietro, the "brains" of our class, who became a doctor, also stood out on the basketball court.

Because Joe Kenneally lived so close to school and I lived as far away as one could get and still qualify to attend the school, I had to take a bus to and from school. When dismissal occurred around 2:15 p.m. at Saint Joseph's School, my siblings and I had to wait over an hour for our bus because the public-school kids, who weren't dismissed until around 3:00 p.m., were picked up first and dropped off at their stops before the bus came for us. Joe, being a good friend, often stayed behind with me to play some games or help the school custodian clean the classrooms. The custodian was a large man around six feet tall or taller with blondish-brown hair and a strong build. At least, that's how he appeared to me as a young fifth or sixth grader.

It was not unusual for Joe and me to assist the custodian with cleaning blackboards, slapping dust off erasers, or using the mop to clean the papers and other garbage off the floors. The custodian was a friendly man who was well-liked by the students and staff. One particular day, however, he became a terrorizing predator. He took me to the teachers' lounge across the hall from his work room well after school had ended and sexually abused me. I recalled the memory around 2013 and reported it to my therapist and attorney.

As I woke up on the morning of my memory returning, I had a feeling of terror come upon me. I lay in bed scared to death while the memory of the custodian overcame me. He took me from the fifth-grade classroom where I was working on cleaning blackboards down the hall into the teachers' lounge. He sat in an office chair with wheels and placed me on his lap. He opened his pants and exposed his penis and then opened my pants and pulled out my penis. I was forced to place my mouth on his penis, but I must have put up a fight because I recall him nearly strangling me to keep me still. He put two hands around my neck and then pulled my head down toward his penis. I was forced to give him oral sex. He then sodomized me. I recall something similar happening to Joe Kenneally. I think I was first and Joe was second. I don't recall if he retrieved Joe from the classroom after he was finished with me or if Joe was in the room with me from the beginning. In any case, Joe appeared in my regained memory that same morning.

I have no memory of the after-events of the sexual abuse. I suppose I retrieved my book bag and waited for my bus. Joe must have gotten his belongings from the fifth-grade class and begun to walk home. I don't remember ever discussing the event with Joe or anyone else. Joe had a very difficult life, fighting serious bouts of depression and dying at a young age—only 60. I attended his funeral and wondered if his life was altered ever since the time he was in grammar school. Joe never married and suffered physical illnesses as well as mental illness. He died of cancer, but fought it a good part of his life. Despite his hardships, he had become a fabulous athlete, both in basketball and golf. He won his country club's golf championship at least one year.

Joe's brother was and is a good friend of my older brother and they both are superb golfers. My brother, a lefty, was an excellent golfer himself and played every chance he got at his golf club in New Jersey, often playing with former Yankee legend Yogi Berra.

I phoned my older brother one day and asked him, "Would you mind phoning Joe Kenneally's brother to ask him if his brother Joe ever confided in him that he had been sexually abused by anyone as a child, specifically personnel at St. Joseph's Parish?" My brother agreed and made the phone call. Joe's brother told my brother that Joe never said anything to him that he had been sexually abused as a child or any other time. Joe attended a Catholic high school in the city. He didn't think Joe was abused by a priest in high school, either.

Joe Kenneally's funeral was held at his parish in 2002 in the pretty little town where he lived by himself in a condominium for many years. He served his parish by coaching several CYO (Catholic Youth Organization) basketball teams for children of many ages, which he loved doing. He was an excellent basketball player at our grammar school, and he played at his high school as well. He became very close to our parish priest, Father Robert Bergen, and Father Bergen was very friendly with the Kenneally family. However, Father Bergen was conspicuously absent from Joe's funeral. He never missed a major sacramental event of the families he endeared himself to, and I wondered during Joe's funeral if Father Bergen was missing because he did something to Joe. A priest from Joe's high school concelebrated Joe's funeral with the pastor, but Father Bergen was nowhere to be found.

Robert M. Hoatson, Ph.D.

The reason for my wonderment was rooted in my regained memory of having been sexually abused by Father Robert Bergen at Taylor's Dairy, a hamburger and ice cream store in a nearby town, on a beautiful Sunday afternoon when I was approximately twelve years old. After my mother died in 2014, whose funeral was conducted by Father Bergen, I received the memory. Taylor's Dairy, which was eventually replaced by upscale homes, was located next door to the town's high school and was a famous hangout for teenagers. Father Bergen often took boys from St. Joseph's Parish to Taylor's Dairy and another famous ice cream store, Bond's, one town away, for similar meals. I was jealous of my brothers, one older and one younger, because Father Bergen took them to those places, and I was always overlooked. My brothers were much better athletes than I was, so I think Father Bergen had a habit of taking the better players to Taylor's and Bond's. Joe Kenneally was another athlete who was often taken on trips for meals with Father Bergen.

While Father Bergen and I were alone at Taylor's Dairy (I thought for sure one of my teammates or brothers would have been invited to come along), he went inside to get hamburgers, fries, and shakes. However, just before he went inside, he leaned over to me in the passenger seat and felt my penis over my clothes. Then, he opened his door and walked inside. I was nervous but thought it may have been a mistake on his part. When he returned to his car, which was parked under an enormous, gorgeous tree overlooking the graveled parking lot, he gave me my food, and we ate together. I thought I was safe since we spent some time eating. I was not safe, though. When we finished eating and the garbage was disposed of, Father Bergen got back into his car (a sedan like a Buick or a Chevrolet), and he once again rubbed my penis over my clothes, then opened my zipper and pulled out my penis. He gave me oral sex as I sat uncomfortably in the passenger seat, worried that someone might see us. When he was done, he opened his own zippered pants and removed his penis. He directed my head down toward his lap and forced me to give him oral sex. I have no memory of anything after that, except I assume he drove me home. I told no one until my memory returned in 2016 or so, when I brought it to my therapy session with Dr. William Richardson.

I had a very hard time explaining to Dr. Richardson what happened, and he curled his brow in disgust when I described the oral sex. I then asked him if my memory could be true. He responded, "Why not? Why would you have had that particular memory had it not happened?" It then made sense to me that I would have another memory of sexual abuse because of my vulnerability from my early days as a teenager and young adult. It was as if I had a phrase imprinted on my forehead: Abuse Me! Besides, I continued to have several episodes of anxiety and depression, even after dealing with acts of abuse by Christian Brothers and others and had it in the back of my mind that I was sexually abused by more persons than I thought.

Besides the Christian Brothers and the pervert in the department store bathroom, I was sexually abused as a child by my parish priest and school custodian. The thousand-pound boulder that sat on my shoulders practically my entire life began to lift, and it helped that Dr. Richardson never doubted my memories for a moment. He congratulated me for being open to retrieving memories of sexual abuse through my subconscious. I was making great progress in therapy. It was comforting to know that none of it was my fault.

Around the same time (2018), I was instructed by my primary care physician, Dr. Daniel Lee, to make an appointment with an oncologist, Dr. Ashish Khot, because he noticed through a blood test that my body was not making enough platelets. He would not speculate what he suspected. I did see Dr. Khot, and he ordered a biopsy of my hip, which would prove or disprove the existence of Myelodysplastic Syndrome, a leukemia type of cancer. The biopsy confirmed Dr. Khot's suspicions, and he referred me to a national expert in the disease at Memorial Sloan Kettering Cancer Hospital in New York City, Dr. Eytan Stein. I made an appointment to see

Dr. Stein. He agreed with the diagnosis of MDS but claimed that currently, I was a low-risk patient. I learned that my blood platelets should be around 400,000 to 500,000 in number, and mine were approximately 125,000. "Ugh," I said to Dr. Stein, "how can that be good?" He responded, "We really won't treat you until your platelets take a serious dive, and then we have ways to treat you." I thanked him, made my way back to the subway and NJ Transit train, and prayed to God that my two serious diseases, C1Q Nephropathy and MDS, would not rear their ugly heads until I was much, much older. So far, God has answered my prayers. My kidney disease was put into remission through a bombardment of the miracle drug Prednisone. I took my recommended dosage of 80 mg. every other day for several months. The disease went into remission. The MDS has not taken that severe dive of which he warned, and Dr. Stein does not expect it to for many years.

When we were eighth graders, Joe Kenneally invited me to his family's home at the Jersey Shore. I was hesitant because I had a history of bedwetting, which was humiliating to me. I had wet the bed for years, not realizing that my history of childhood sexual abuse was likely the reason. My mother and I came up with an outfit that would at least keep the urine in my pants if I wet the bed. Under my pajamas were not one, but two diapers, one plastic and the other one made of cloth material. I escaped bedwetting that weekend and felt great about it. In fact, it was the last time I worried about wetting the bed. It never happened again after eighth grade. I traveled extensively with my high school debate team, and I never wet a bed. It was a major relief to me. I thought my physical ailments were pretty well over. What I didn't realize was that

I suffered from Post-Traumatic Syndrome, something I have dealt with since I was a young boy.

Speaking of my time as a young boy, I had another memory return around the time of the priest and custodian memory. For years, I played at a West Orange park called Stagg Field. My family belonged to a nearby swim club when I was a third and fourth grader, and I was in my glory. I spent as much time as I could at the pool and participated in its activities as well, including swim meets.

The club also produced "The Sound of Music," and I was chosen to play "Mi," as in Do Re Mi. My mother came up with a perfect costume, and I looked just like the character in the movie. When I wasn't at the club, I walked next door to Stagg Field to participate in summer arts and crafts and sports activities at the park. The person in charge was a very popular and charismatic man by the name of Sal DeRienzo. Sal was beloved by all the kids because of his sterling personality and hard work.

Unfortunately, Sal was a sexual abuser of children, and I was one of his victims. When I went into the recreation building one day to use the bathroom, Sal came in and fondled me when I was in a bathroom stall. My swimming trunks were down around my ankles, and Sal had his way with me after I urinated. I didn't know whether to scream, run, or hit him. I was a little kid then and didn't have a chance against Sal's adult body. I repressed the memory until later in adulthood. I googled Sal DeRienzo's name once my memory returned, and I found he was on a sex offender list in the state of New Jersey.

Robert M. Hoatson, Ph.D.

CHAPTER THIRTY

FROM SUICIDAL VICTIM TO SURVIVOR

Sometime around the early 1980s, one of the lowest periods of my life, I had a heart-to-heart talk with Jesus, a good friend of mine. I had always been enamored with the life of Jesus, and the New Testament has always been one of my favorite books. Through my prayer life as a child, teenager, Christian Brother, deacon, and priest, I could always count on Jesus to answer my prayers. Never did He abandon me; although at times, I thought it might be possible. The heart-to-heart talk I had in the 1980s with Jesus was a Hail Mary pass. I remember crying out, "Jesus, if you get me through this hell, I will dedicate my entire life to you and your mission." Yes, I bartered with Jesus; after all, I learned to bring everything to Jesus and allow Him to take over. One of the Christian Brothers somewhat crudely used to tell young brothers who were struggling, "Chuck it in the chalice." Well, I had to chuck it somewhere, so I gave it all to Jesus in my prayer that day.

One of the thoughts I wanted Jesus to take away from me was that of suicide. While I never believed I would take my own life, I couldn't get the thought out of my mind. Here I was, a religious brother and priest, supposedly spreading the good news of Jesus but struggling to rid myself of horrible thoughts. I was terrified of high places because I was afraid I would lose control and jump. When I used knives in the kitchen, I was fearful that I would lose control and stab someone. When I drove a car and came to a red light, I used to put the car in neutral so I wouldn't suddenly step on the gas and run over the pedestrians crossing the street. And when I crossed bridges like the George Washington, I prayed there would be no traffic jams so I wouldn't be tempted to turn off the ignition and jump off the bridge. Fortunately, I learned through therapy that I was suffering from neurotic thoughts caused by the sexual abuse and the concomitant post-traumatic stress disorder. I no longer have those fears, for the most part.

Having attended numerous support groups and therapy sessions over the course of 50 years, I figured out that I was not alone. Almost everyone I spoke to who was a victim of sexual abuse had some sort of mental and physical illness that permeated their lives and haunted them for years. Fortunately for me, the Christian Brothers and the Archdiocese of Newark had excellent medical insurance, so I was able to remain in therapy all these years. When it came time for me to pay for sessions, I made sure to sacrifice comforts and necessities to remain in therapy. I considered it mandatory for my recovery. I only wish every victim of sexual abuse had the same "perks" that I had. Their lives would have been different.

Who would have thought that Jesus' answer to my prayers in the 1980s would have led me to leave the religious life and the priesthood? My hiring at Sacred Heart High School in 1989 and finding a close friend in Father Philip Fabiano led me to leave the Christian Brothers in 1994. Surprisingly, it led me to the priesthood. Many people I speak to cannot understand how I could have entered a seminary after being sexually abused in the religious life. My answer is the same each time: "I thought I could help reform the church if I became a priest and lived basically as an independent vendor, unlike religious life, where I lived in community with many others." I honestly thought that the diocesan priesthood would keep me safe since I would be more independent—owning my own car, receiving a salary, and determining much of my personal life. Actually, the diocesan priesthood was worse in many ways.

I brought this issue to therapy one day with Dr. Richardson and said to him, an Episcopalian, Harvard-educated agnostic, "I think I need to start a non-profit organization to help victims of sexual abuse." Without blinking an eye, Dr. Richardson responded, "Of course, you do. It will help others and yourself." He was right, as usual. Road to Recovery, Inc. saved my life and convinced me that the priesthood would never afford me the opportunity to truly be a priest. Jesus was keeping his promise, and so was I. He wanted me to help the most needy, including myself, in our recovery from institutional, sexual, and psychological abuse. Therefore, in 2011, I petitioned Pope Benedict XVI to allow me to leave the priesthood, and I received my laicization papers in nine months—no doubt a record. When they want you out, they move quickly. Archbishop Myers made sure of that.

Robert M. Hoatson, Ph.D.

CHAPTER THIRTY-ONE

MURDER, HE WROTE

It was Palm Sunday, 2011. The parishioners of Immaculate Conception Parish, Newark, NJ, had gathered for the 9:00 a.m. Sunday liturgy on one of the most crowded days of the Church calendar. Palm Sunday is one of the feasts on which C.A.P.E. Catholics attend Mass in huge numbers. C.A.P.E. refers to "Christmas, Ashes, Palms, and Easter," the days that cafeteria Catholics expect to re-introduce themselves to the Catholic Mass. Many priests use those days to remind the congregations that their parishes are open every Sunday and it would be nice to see them more often. Some clergy do so politely while others scold the infrequent attendees. Since Immaculate Conception Church was not a large church, there was an overflow crowd there that Palm Sunday and many Catholics heard the priest's sermon that morning.

Immaculate Conception Parish had recently merged with Our Lady of Good Counsel Parish, a few blocks south, but both churches would remain open, Immaculate Conception for Sunday Masses only. Our Lady of Good Counsel was the larger of the two parishes, so it had a full complement of programs and activities. At one point, Immaculate Conception was a parish founded by and made up of Italian immigrants, but most of those parishioners had moved west of the city to tonier suburbs. Puerto Rican and Cuban immigrants had taken the Italians' place, and Immaculate Conception had become a mostly Spanish-speaking parish. It was at the time of the transition in the middle to late 1970s that Fr. Jude Ippolito was ordained a priest and was assigned to Immaculate Conception Parish as his first priestly assignment. In addition, the pastor of the parish was of Italian descent, so despite the Hispanic influence moving in, the Archdiocese continued to send Italian pastors and priests to serve there.

Robert M. Hoatson, Ph.D.

Shortly after the 9:00 am Mass on that Palm Sunday in 2011, I received a telephone call from Sammy Rivera, a sexual abuse victim of Fr. Jude Ippolito at Immaculate Conception Parish. He told me his cousin, Jaime, had attended the 9:00 am Mass and reported that Fr. John Connor, during his Palm Sunday homily, said words to the effect that "if I were Fr. Jude Ippolito, I would have those guys who accused him of sexual abuse murdered, including that priest who leads them." That priest was I.

When Sammy Rivera finished telling me his cousin's account of Palm Sunday Mass, I suggested to him that the two of us should go to the north station of the police department and report the threat that Fr. Connor had issued. I picked up Sammy Rivera in my car and we headed to the police department. An officer spoke to us but concluded that he could not do anything about it because Fr. Connor did not issue a direct threat that HE was going to murder us. He simply said that we should be murdered.

Four days later, on Holy Thursday, Sammy Rivera and I arrived with other clergy sexual abuse victims to conduct a peaceful, public demonstration outside Immaculate Conception Church. Shortly after we arrived and began to unload our placards and other materials, Fr. Connor walked from the rectory across the parking lot to unlock the gate to the stairway which led to the church. While he was unchaining the gate, Sammy said, "Hey Father, here we are, you want us dead, right?"

Fr. Connor turned around and said to Sammy, "Oh, I didn't mean you. I meant that priest over there (me). He should be murdered for causing so much trouble." Needless to say, I could not call the police since Fr. Connor had not directly threatened me, but we commenced and continued our demonstration. Some parishioners, no doubt taking bad example from the priest, verbally and nearly assaulted us as we peacefully and quietly demonstrated.

The reason for our demonstration on Holy Thursday was to draw parishioners' and neighbors' attention to the sexual abuse that took place at Immaculate Conception Parish by Fr. Jude Ippolito. Several months previously, a young man named Ernie approached me to say that he was sexually abused by three men. His heroic reporting led to the uncovering of a large number of victims of Fr. Jude at Immaculate Conception Parish.

Recall that Our Lady of Good Counsel Parish and Immaculate Conception Parish were only a few blocks from each other, and both parishes became populated by large numbers of Hispanic populations moving into the area from Puerto Rico, Cuba, Mexico, and the Dominican Republic. Ernie had a relationship with both parishes since he lived closer to Immaculate Conception but participated in sacramental and athletic programs at Our Lady of Good Counsel, where he met the deacon/coach and priest who sexually abused him.

Ernie's reports of sexual abuse prompted other Hispanic men from the area to begin their journeys toward healing. I met with four other victims of Fr. Jude Ippolito in a local Hispanic restaurant in the area, and each of them told horrific stories of sexual touching of the underarms and other parts of the body, being drugged and made to sleep in Fr. Jude's bed at the Jersey Shore, and not wanting to sit in the passenger seat of his car as they rode to a gymnasium because he would engage in unwanted touching and pinching.

Frequently, Fr. Jude would take a car full of parish boys to the Jersey Shore, and then serve them soda. In one of the soda cups, according to more than one victim, was what they described as a "date night" drug or similar drug that made the boys woozy and dizzy. The boy chosen for a given night woke up with soiled underwear and pains in his rectum and/or elsewhere. A weekend at the beach became a two-day hell for whomever was selected to sleep with Fr. Jude, who chose different boys on different days.

Two of the victims of Fr. Jude were brothers who lived diagonally across from the rectory. They were children of immigrants from Puerto Rico and one was better looking than the other. These boys became Fr. Jude's "playmates" as they were often summoned to the rectory to help with parish business, serve at the altar for funerals and weddings, or simply to go for rides in Fr. Jude's car. One of the brothers died in his early '40s of a massive heart attack. He had become morbidly obese and tried to survive his trauma by himself because his brother went off the deep end after the abuse. He began to take drugs and they kept him on the streets and in prison for most of his life. His brain was literally "fried" and he spent each and every day going to an outpatient facility for those who could not function on their own. Today, he is back on the streets after receiving a settlement and misusing those funds which drove him back to risky behavior.

Because of the hard work of advocates and attorneys, the older brother, despite being deceased, was the recipient of a settlement which went to his mother who had tried for decades to keep her sons alive. She, unfortunately, had a case of Alzheimer's and tragically passed away. This tragedy is the norm, not the exception, for most victim/survivors. The stress of the trauma creates challenges not just for the victims but families and friends alike.

Fr. Jude Ippolito lured children into the Immaculate Conception Parish rectory by showing them the train set that was set up by the pastor in one of the rectory rooms. The parents of the children, mainly boys, had no idea what was happening to their kids. It is called grooming. What Fr. Jude was doing was grooming them into thinking it was "cool" to hang out with the priests of the parish, especially Fr. Jude. The cadre of boys who were groomed, then sexually abused, at Immaculate Conception Parish numbered at least a dozen and a half, including some boys who were sexually abused before, during, or after religious education classes. One parent purportedly threatened Fr. Jude Ippolito with physical harm after Fr. Jude pulled the underarm hair of his son while the boy was in class.

Fr. Jude Ippolito was a favored priest of the Archbishop. He was sent to another parish in the city where his behavior may have continued, but shortly thereafter, he became pastor of a large and wealthy suburban parish. One Saturday afternoon, while several of us victims and advocates demonstrated outside the parish alerting parishioners to Fr. Jude's history of sexual abuse of minor children, a woman approached us to say that her husband, the former police chief of the town, was a very close friend of Fr. Jude and supposedly looked the other way when he received allegations against Fr. Jude. Despite the number of claims and substantiated allegations against Fr. Jude, the Archbishop refused to remove him from ministry.

Fr. Jude Ippolito was re-assigned from that parish to take over as pastor of an even larger and wealthier parish in the suburbs. Every weekend, a number of Ippolito victims and I demonstrated peacefully outside the confines of the parish, but some parishioners were violent and arrogant. One man pulled his truck over, jumped out screaming at us, and the local policeman, who was assigned to guard us, told the guy to get back into his truck. He was an employee of the town. Another elderly woman unintentionally lost control of her car and headed toward us as we stood on the footpath near the driveway. Despite all this evidence and possible injury to innocent persons, the Archbishop refused to remove Fr. Jude Ippolito from ministry.

It wasn't until several weeks later that Fr. Jude Ippolito purportedly was allowed to retire with full pension and benefits. Around that time, a parishioner of a parish where Fr. Jude was stationed informed me that she saw Fr. Jude driving his convertible (evidently he had two or more cars to lure kids to him) with several 11-14 year old boys in the car. She saw him park the car at a local supermarket and left the kids in the car as he ran in to the store to buy something. Her own son was an altar server at the church and she was very concerned because he had been abused by a relative of his as a young child.

Robert M. Hoatson, Ph.D.

CHAPTER THIRTY-TWO

LEAVING THE PRIESTHOOD AND BLOWING THE WHISTLE – AGAIN

November, 2011, was a difficult month for me. I loved being a priest, especially when I said Mass and preached, but I knew there was no way that I could stay and function with integrity. I would have had to compromise my conscience, and I wasn't willing to do that. Besides, I was thrilled to be able to do my work with Road to Recovery, Inc. without having anyone looking over my shoulder and judging my work as being disloyal or rebellious. I began to do a lot more demonstrating and leafleting at parishes and other Catholic institutions regarding clergy sexual abuse.

I fortunately held things together in my life. The longer I was out of the priesthood, the more comfortable I was in repeating what a priest friend of mine used to say after his retirement: "I don't work for that company anymore." We laughed together whenever we spoke on the telephone. He was the priest, Patrick Collins, who converted to Catholicism and worked in a diocese in the Midwest with Bishop Myers but left when Myers became bishop. He purchased himself a little house in Michigan that he called his hermitage.

I wrote to Archbishop Myers at the beginning of 2011 and expressed my desire to leave the priesthood. He was thrilled to hear the news. In his letter back to me, he said he would be happy to write a letter to the Vatican recommending that Pope Benedict allow me to get out of the priesthood quickly. I received my laicization papers the day before Thanksgiving, 2011, so it took less than a year for Myers to get me out. Most times, the pedophiles remain for years or forever. When they want you out, they get you out. The nine months it took for my process of laicization had to be a record. Of course, Archbishop Myers never showed me his letter to the Vatican, but it must have been a doozy.

Myers knew exactly what to do to get me out as soon as possible, and he rubbed it in by sending me my laicization papers on Thanksgiving Eve. That showed how unfeeling he was. He couldn't wait until after the Thanksgiving or even the Christmas holidays to send the paperwork, which was in Latin, very comprehensive, and difficult to pore through. Myers also sent me a list of things I could or couldn't do as an ex-priest, such as not being able to teach theology in a Catholic university, high school, or elementary school. He did tell me I could get married. Imagine: they even want to control you when you're no longer a priest.

After I was laicized and out of the priesthood permanently, I think Archbishop Myers must have had second thoughts about my leaving the priesthood because I became a bigger thorn in his side after I left than before. I was free now to do whatever needed to be done to expose the cover-up of clergy sexual abuse in the Archdiocese of Newark, and it was extensive, to say the least. I began to follow the case of Father Michael Fugee, a priest who was credibly accused of sexually abusing a minor at St. Elizabeth Parish, Wyckoff, NJ in a wealthy suburb in northern New Jersey. Father Fugee, instead of being defrocked or removed permanently from ministry, was allowed by Archbishop Myers to become a hospital chaplain in Newark and then a staff member of the Propagation of the Faith for the archdiocese with an office in headquarters. His job was essentially to collect funds from the children of archdiocesan schools and other programs.

Needless to say, I contacted a reporter for the *Newark Star Ledger*, Jeff Diamant, and he began his investigative report. He found that Fugee was at St. Michael's Hospital in Newark, NJ as a chaplain (the hospital had a pediatric ward), and he questioned the archdiocese about that. Then Father Fugee ended up in the office of the Propagation of the Faith, and the reporter questioned that.

Each time, the archdiocese had tried to stay ahead of the media and those of us who were following this cover-up.

Finally, Fugee was allowed to live in Holy Family Parish rectory, Nutley, NJ, with his friend Monsignor Paul Bochicchio. While there, Father Fugee worked with the youth of the parish and heard confessions as well. In addition, he and two friends of his from St. Mary's Parish, Colts Neck, NJ, located in a different diocese, welcomed Father Fugee to work with the youth group there and hear confessions of young people at that parish. The pastor of Saint Mary's Parish was removed as pastor of his parish, and the pastor of Holy Family Parish was also removed for a time.

Law enforcement authorities throughout New Jersey followed these developments very carefully because Father Fugee was not supposed to be around children at all based on a memorandum of understanding between the state attorney general's office and the bishops of New Jersey. Law enforcement came down hard on Archbishop Myers and his vicar general, Monsignor John Doran, who also lost his job as a result of the mismanagement of the Fugee case. The archdiocese was instructed to defrock (laicize) Father Fugee or expect criminal charges to be filed. Throughout this entire process, I worked with the media, whose reports pressured the Archdiocese of Newark to finally do the right thing in the Fugee case. But there were hundreds of other cases that the Newark Archdiocese had covered up that came to my knowledge, and we did not let up with our advocacy and support for victims.

Robert M. Hoatson, Ph.D.

CHAPTER THIRTY-THREE

FREEDOM FROM THE MAFIA

My new life as a lay person felt like I had been released from prison. Except for my federal lawsuit in 2005, I had never challenged Archbishop Myers' decisions and disciplines because I knew whatever I tried would be heard before a kangaroo court, especially during the time I was whistleblowing.

My career in the Archdiocese of Newark was finished when I stood up to Myers, and I wasn't even able go to another diocese since the sending bishop, Myers, would have had to write a letter of recommendation to the receiving bishop. I had written to Archbishop McCarrick in Washington, DC, to ask him to allow me to switch dioceses. He wrote back and told me to obey Archbishop Myers, and all would work out fine for me in the Archdiocese of Newark. As I look back, it was like writing to the head of the Gambino family, asking to join the Genovese family.

Robert M. Hoatson, Ph.D.

CHAPTER THIRTY-FOUR

I KEPT MY PROMISE, AND JESUS KEPT HIS

By the time I was laicized by the Vatican, Road to Recovery, Inc. had been in business for nearly ten years. The non-profit began in the studio apartment I escaped to in Rockaway Beach, and what an oasis it was. Apartment 9-F was nine stories above the Atlantic Ocean, with panoramic views from an outdoor deck. At times, I thought I would be knocked out of bed from the noises of huge jets taking off from Kennedy Airport and flying right over my building. I seldom had to use air conditioning, as the breezes from the ocean wafted through the apartment almost every day.

When I exercised, I took a several-mile walk along the boardwalk and occasionally headed to the beach to do some swimming and sunbathing. However, the phone calls from victims were coming in at a rate of five to ten per day in the early days, and these men and women needed lots of help. I was working between twelve and sixteen hours per day, and since we advertised that our "phone was always on," I often received calls in the middle of the night because most victims have erratic sleeping patterns, including me.

My work with victims intensified once I was fired from my ministry at Our Lady of Good Counsel Schools in Newark. Legally, Road to Recovery, Inc. was allowed to request tax deductible funds, and the donations began to flow in. At first, our success occurred due to word of mouth, but then I began to send letters to family, friends, parishioners, and others who I thought might support our work.

My travels took me to many states and countries, and I quickly put hundreds of thousands of miles on my Ford Taurus. I was still being paid by the Newark Archdiocese, so I did not take a salary from Road to Recovery. By canon law, the Archbishop of Newark had to support me because I was still a priest. My medical and car insurance was still paid by the archdiocese and lasted until I left the priesthood in 2011, when I began taking a salary from the non-profit.

Road to Recovery also began to pay for my medical, car, malpractice, and workmen's compensation insurance. It has done so to the present, thanks to the Board of Directors. My modest salary combined with my very modest Social Security monthly payment permits me to live much more comfortably than many Americans who have no jobs, food, or hope.

In 2019, I attended the SNAP (Survivor's Network of Those Abused by Priests) Conference in Washington, DC, as I did every year, no matter where it was held. I think I may have missed one conference since 2003, but I enjoy seeing my fellow victims, hearing good talks, and socializing with hundreds of people from around the world. Sunday morning came, and I was attending the final session of the weekend. Usually, I leave around the middle of the morning session, but this time, I stayed until the very end. Good thing, because I was awarded SNAP's 2019 award for my service to sexual abuse victims all these years. I was shocked and barely able to speak when my name was announced.

Around the same time as the announcement of the SNAP award, I heard by telephone from two members of the Essex Catholic High School Hall of Fame who requested that I consider accepting induction into the Hall of Fame because of my "heroic" work with clergy sexual abuse victims. They told me that the Hall of Fame had expelled Archbishop Theodore McCarrick and Father Jude Ippolito because of their sexual abuse of minor children, and they thought they should finally honor someone who has been fighting for justice for decades. I was not very cordial at first with these men because I had already petitioned my high school Hall of Fame for assistance with victims, especially my cousin who committed suicide, Jimmy Craig Hoatson. I asked the Hall of Fame to honor my cousin posthumously as a signal to victims that there were people on their side. Besides, Jimmy's mother, Alice, was still alive at 93, and I thought it might help her recover from the trauma of losing her son due to sexual abuse at Essex Catholic High School by Brother Jerome Heustis.

I finally accepted the invitation of the Board of the Essex Catholic High School Alumni Association to be inducted, and on November 20, 2020, five of us alumni were inducted, along with members of the track team and drama club. I was asked to deliver the invocation and then a five-minute acceptance speech. I finished my talk proclaiming that my love affair with Essex Catholic High School from 1966–1970 culminated at commencement in 1970 when I was presented with the school's most prestigious award, "The Most Outstanding Senior Award." It exemplified my love for the school and the school's love for me. In a few months following graduation, I would enter the Christian Brothers and begin a life of service in the Church. At least, that's what my idealism had in mind.

Because of my history of sexual abuse by many persons, I developed "abuse radar," and for decades, I have been able to determine whether or not certain adults are preying on children. I have catalogued in my brain behaviors and verbiage used by predators to sexually abuse children, teenagers, and vulnerable adults. I was sexually abused during all three of those stages of life, and the pain and suffering in all three is basically the same. Shame, guilt, depression, anxiety, and PTSD permeate the brain, making it difficult to focus, concentrate, think, and act. We victims spend many days and nights in turmoil. Oftentimes, our brains do not stop spinning, and strong medicines are needed to reach some form of stability. As I write this book, I am taking medicines for depression and anxiety. I haven't been on medicines all my life, but it's comforting to know they are there when needed.

Robert M. Hoatson, Ph.D.

One of the interesting aspects of my life and the lives of many victim/survivors of sexual abuse is the number of places I have lived. I was born in 1952, the second born in the family. For the first eighteen years of life, I lived essentially in two different houses in the same town. However, I never thought that I would have twenty-seven changes in residence in 70 years. That includes the ten years I have been living in my current federal and state-subsidized senior apartment building in my hometown. When my mother died in 2014, her will indicated that I could live in the family home until I died, but I didn't need an entire house to live in by myself. So, I registered for senior housing and was accepted immediately. My four siblings and I sold the family home in 2014. I have a one-bedroom apartment on the eighth floor of the senior apartment building that overlooks one of the state's busy highways. It is very convenient for my frequent travels in and out of state.

My father, Archie, died in 2010. His wake was held at a funeral home in the local town where he grew up and was an all-state football player and a very fine basketball player. He was offered a partial scholarship to the College of William and Mary to play football, but he joined the Marines instead. He fought in the Pacific and lost some of his hearing because he was a communications specialist. Bombs often blew up in his ears while he relayed and accepted orders from the superior officers. The line at his wake wound around the funeral home and out into the parking lot.

My father was not Catholic, so his funeral arrangements were a bit complicated. He was not a church goer, but I was still a priest, and my family thought we should have a religious ceremony of some sort for him. My mother, of course, was in favor of a prayer service and a military burial. I requested of the archdiocese that we use the mausoleum at the Catholic cemetery where they had purchased a grave for two to hold a prayer service. My siblings and I led the service, and my niece and nephew provided the music. Father Robert Bergen attended, as did Father Philip Concannon, with whom I served at Holy Trinity Parish in Bergen County. The mausoleum accommodated approximately one hundred people, and most chairs were filled. Father Bergen liked my father very much because he was an excellent carpenter and did a number of jobs for St. Joseph's Parish, including painting the parish hall, making renovations to the old building, and rebuilding Father Bergen's private bathroom in Mooney Hall on the campus of Seton Hall University when Father Bergen was named to the faculty of Seton Hall Prep. On every major holiday for sixty years, Father Bergen phoned my parents to greet them and wish them well. After the funeral and a military tribute, we took my father a few hundred yards to the plot purchased for him and my mother. She would join him there four years later.

My siblings were relieved that someone from the family was living with our parents, and they expressed their appreciation often. They would call and tell me to take a day off while they took care of Mom and Dad, and I usually would make a beeline for Broadway and see a show. Broadway has been my favorite thing to do since 1968 when I saw my first musical, "1776," and my first drama, "Child's Play." I was hooked. I try to see as many Broadway shows as possible. How do I afford those prices? I go to the half-price booth or I buy standing room only tickets (I am getting a bit old to stand throughout an entire show, however) or I go to the box office for reduced price tickets called "Rush" tickets. I am also a member of the "Theater Development Fund" (TDF), which sells great seats at reduced prices. I never pay full price for a Broadway ticket.

The pandemic closed Broadway for over a year, and I suffered withdrawal symptoms. I am thrilled that Times Square is once again teeming with theatergoers. Keep in mind that I lived in Hell's Kitchen for nearly six years and was able to get into Broadway shows for free because many of our parishioners at Sacred Heart of Jesus Parish were ushers and usherettes, grips, actors, producers, and longshoreman, so the connections were plentiful. I also was able to attend a few Tony Award dress rehearsals when I lived in the theater district.

My mother died in April, 2014. I had gotten up in the middle of the night to check on her, and she seemed to be struggling with her hydration. I fed her some ice chips and knew it wouldn't be long before she breathed her last breath. I was tempted to call my siblings at that time, around 3:00 a.m., but I figured she would last until early morning at least. I was wrong. I went back to bed, and when I woke up at 6:00 a.m. or so, I went into her room, and she was gone. I phoned my three brothers and one sister and the hospice staff, which was wonderful for the two or so months we had them. Unfortunately, the siblings could not say their final goodbyes, but they had been at the house the day before because of her weakened condition. My sister volunteered to go to the funeral home with her husband to make the arrangements. That was fine with all of us since she was very close to my mother.

My mother was buried from her parish church where she worshiped since the parish opened in the late 1950s. The church building was completed in 1962, and I served the first Mass in the church at midnight on Christmas Eve, 1962. The heat had not yet been installed, so the pastor ordered commercial heaters so we wouldn't freeze. The pastor was a popular man who replaced the founding pastor after he had some medical issues shortly after being named. Father Tom Mulquinn was a sickly man but served the people well. He was replaced by an eccentric priest who allegedly ran off with all the rectory's accoutrements when he retired. He used to direct traffic after each Mass just like a traffic cop, and his heavy "Joisey" accent often left us in stitches. His "deliver us from all turmoil" at Mass came out as "deliver us from all toomerl." The next pastor, Monsignor G. Thomas Burns, was universally loved and remained for many years until his retirement. He retired to Florida. My father, a non-Catholic, particularly liked Monsignor Burns because he welcomed my father whenever there was a family ritual or Mass.

Our favorite priest of all at St. Raphael's was Father John Madden because he gave the shortest homilies on record, I think. After he read the Gospel, he would say, "Please remain standing," and he would deliver a one-or-two-minute homily (at the most) and then get on with the Mass. He was down to earth and treated everyone with kindness. When it came time for elections for the Grand Knight of the Altar (altar boys), I was nominated and selected. What did it mean? I couldn't tell you, except that I probably served more Masses at that parish than any altar boy ever.

When I was in the eighth grade at St. Joseph's School (our new parish's school had not yet been built), I attended the "Vocations Fair" in the Seton Hall University gymnasium. The entire gym was filled with nuns, priests, and brothers who were recruiting candidates for their religious orders or diocesan priesthoods. I had a bag full of cards of interest by the end of the afternoon, and I filled out dozens of them and mailed them off to the religious orders. Within a few weeks, a priest from the Carmelite order arrived at our house to offer me a spot in the high school seminary of the Carmelites out of state. My mother and I sat with him for a few minutes, but my mother was determined. She told the priest, "Thank you for coming, Father, but Bobby will not be going anywhere until at least after high school." That was that. I was glad she told him that, although the prospect of becoming a priest was attractive to me. I received bags of literature in the mail asking me to consider the brotherhood and priesthood. I didn't get anything from nuns' religious orders, thank goodness.

Robert M. Hoatson, Ph.D.

CHAPTER THIRTY-FIVE

HEROES GOVERNOR FRANK KEATING AND ATTORNEY MITCHELL GARABEDIAN

Frank Keating, the former governor of Oklahoma, was tapped by the National Conference of Catholic Bishops (the name changed to the United States Conference of Catholic Bishops) in 2002 to become the first chairperson of the National Review Board for the Protection of Children and Young People. He was joined by other well-known Catholics, such as Justice Anne Burke of Illinois and famed lawyer Robert Bennett of Washington, DC. Once the "charter" was adopted at the Dallas meeting of bishops, the National Review Board was constituted to hold the bishops accountable for their promises of openness, transparency, truthfulness, and honesty. Bishop Wilton Gregory of Belleville, Illinois, at the time, President of the Bishops' Conference, later to become Archbishop of Atlanta and now Cardinal Archbishop of Washington, DC, foolishly announced at the press conference releasing the charter that the crisis of clergy sexual abuse was over. I knew trouble was ahead because nothing really changed relative to the approach taken by the bishops.

Governor Frank Keating agreed with me and resigned as chair of the National Review Board within a year of his taking office. He compared working with the United States Bishops as dealing with the Mafia, "with all due respect to the Mafia" (these are my words). He was ordered by cardinals like Roger Mahony of Los Angeles (who would be disgraced years later after his cover-ups in the Archdiocese of Los Angeles and the Diocese of Santa Rosa were made public) to retract his comments, but he refused and resigned instead. What courage for Governor Keating to stick to his guns and make known and confirm what many of us have known for decades. The Church hierarchy is corrupt to the core and needs to be dismantled. Church royalty has to go. Jesus never intended his Church to be a Mafia-like institution. Since 2002, nothing has changed in the American or international Catholic Church, and clergy sexual abuse will continue to ravage children's lives and those of teenagers and vulnerable adults precisely because Pope Francis never had the guts to make the changes necessary. He knew what had to happen but wouldn't take the risk. He talked a good game but got nothing done.

Since Governor Keating's resignation as the first Chairperson of the National Review Board, he has held a number of positions in the public and private sectors, and he seems to have maintained his high moral standards. Unfortunately, the same cannot be said of the United States Bishops. Attorney Mitchell Garabedian perhaps says it best at press conferences and other gatherings. He claims that the Catholic Church, purportedly the most moral institution in the world, mostly acts immorally, at least when it comes to clergy sexual abuse. Governor Keating, I suspect, would agree.

As mentioned in an earlier chapter, I have been working closely and collaboratively with an attorney from Boston, Mitchell Garabedian, who, like several other people, was placed in my life by God. Attorney Garabedian is one of the most ethical, moral, loyal, compassionate, and empathetic persons I have ever met. He is solid as a rock in approaching the law and all other matters. He and I have worked so well together because we have the same standards. We are committed to helping victim/survivors and speaking truth to power. Church authorities in Boston attempted numerous times to have him disbarred for speaking the truth, and they failed each and every time. He and I share similarities in that I was fired from ministry and lost my cherished career as a priest, and he had to protect his ministry of practicing the law honestly and without malice. Sean Brady and Bobby Martin introduced me to Mr. Garabedian in 2002, and now, over two decades later, our shared commitment to victim/survivors and justice for them continues.

On August 7, 2019, my attorney, Mitchell Garabedian, and I held a press conference at a hotel in my hometown, where I announced that I had been sexually abused by Father Robert Bergen as a child. I had done hundreds of press conferences and demonstrations over the years, but I was never as nervous as I was that day. My attorney even asked me if I wanted to go through with it because he could tell by my voice that I was feeling weak. Within minutes of my announcement, the media had photos of Father Bergen on their phones and asked me to identify him, which I did. Going public with an allegation for the first time without having any corroboration from others is very traumatic. I was sure, however, that there were more victims of Father Bergen.

Within one day, another victim of Father Bergen phoned me to say that he had been sexually abused by Bergen at St. Joseph's rectory for two years. "John Doe" said to me, "Bob, my name is 'John Doe,' and I want to thank you for your courage in announcing that Father Bergen sexually abused you because he sexually abused me, too." I asked him if he wanted to tell me what happened. "Sure," he responded, "Bergen took me into his suite of rooms for two years and sexually abused me." My knees began to buckle, and I thought I was going to faint. "Two years?" I shockingly repeated. "Yes," he said. "When Monsignor Fitzsimmons took his weekly day off, Father Bergen would take me to his rooms and abuse me. Sometimes it happened more than once a week."

"Monsignor Fitzsimmons' sister had a house in the lake region of northwest New Jersey, and he visited her fairly frequently. He also took his vacations there as well. For two years, Bergen trapped me in his room on his bed. He made me strip and then put on a speedo and then told me to get into his bed."

I wanted to cry. He told me he played basketball for St. Joseph's School and was on a team with one of my brothers. I didn't remember him, but he said he remembered me. We then reminisced about St. Joseph's School and speculated about other possible victims. I then said to him, "I was also sexually abused by the school custodian, and I suspect that Joe Kenneally may have been abused right after me in the teachers' lounge as I waited for my bus after school." John Doe jumped in, "What? The custodian was very close to my parents, and he and my father had an interest in birds. They were very friendly." John Doe then told me, "And Bergen was very close to my parents as well. He often had dinner in my house, and my parents invited him frequently to visit. My father was in the medical profession and took care of Bergen."

"Holy shit," I responded, "both of our families were affected by the custodian and Bergen. That can't be coincidental."

Child sexual abusers often befriend families, like Bergen and the custodian did with us. "The custodian was not as friendly with my family, I suspect, because we lived a fair distance from the school." I then told him what he had also done to me. "He got me in the teachers' lounge, and he sat in one of the chairs on wheels. He sat me on his lap, and I must have tried to wriggle away because he grabbed me by the throat and nearly strangled me. He then opened his pants, took out his penis, and made me perform oral sex on him. It was excruciating. He then opened my zipper and performed oral sex on me."

"John Doe" offered his sympathy and then told me what he did about his sexual abuse. He said, "I contacted the Archdiocese and reported Father Bergen. I gave them details of his rooms, his bed, his suite furniture, and the rectory's first and second floors. They found me credible. I told them I didn't want any money, but I wanted Bergen's name to be removed from St. Stephen's Academy Hall of Fame and the dugout donated by a professional baseball player who graduated from St. Stephen's Academy. They have yet to answer me. I may have to join you, Bob, in demonstrating against them if they don't give me what I want. Ironically, even though I didn't ask for money, they mailed me a check."

Since I heard from John Doe, a local woman stopped by to say that her two sons were abused by Father Bergen, and another victim has come forward as well. That means five sexual abuse victims of Father Bergen have come forward and we expect more to emerge.

As I mentioned in an earlier chapter, my claim was denied by the Independent Victim's Compensation Program because they (the law firm of Kenneth Feinberg) could not corroborate my report, even though they had already interviewed "John Doe" and found him credible. I was victim #2, at least. I was interviewed at length by telephone by Administrator Camille Biros, and my attorney submitted evidence of my memories, including reports from my therapists, William Richardson, MD, and Benedict Vicarisi, LMFT, LPC. As soon as the memories of Father Bergen and that custodian came back to me, I reported them to Dr. Richardson, and he believed me.

Frightening aspects of Father Bergen's career were not considered years ago because most Catholics considered him to be a humble priest, which he was in many ways. His car was totaled in the 1960s in an accident, and the parishioners purchased him a new car. He was not happy about it because it embarrassed him. He accepted the gift thankfully but not happily. His humility may have been covering up a nefarious aspect of his personality. I was told years ago that Father Bergen phoned all the freshmen at St. Stephen's Academy on their birthdays, and he held "spiritual" counseling sessions with every freshman in a guidance-type office every year as well, particularly in the years after he was retired from teaching full-time. It is frightening to think that he would have phoned and counseled thousands of unsuspecting St. Stephen's Academy students during his years there. It is widely known most sexual abusers have many victims, not just five, so an educated guess would indicate that there are many more victims of Father Robert Bergen.

Robert M. Hoatson, Ph.D.

CHAPTER THIRTY-SIX

WHAT IS WRONG WITH THIS PICTURE?

There is something very wrong with the Roman Catholic Church, and it must be fixed. For centuries, children have been sexually abused by clergy, and the introduction of mandatory celibacy in the Middle Ages was a disaster. Mandating that men must not marry or engage in sex at any time in their lives as priests has created a tragedy beyond measure. When you ask human beings to do something unnatural, they are bound to act unnaturally. Many men are called to the priesthood, but not to mandatory celibacy. In the 1970s, in particular, men and women in religious life and the priesthood left in droves because the freedom and refreshment that Vatican II (ending in the mid-1960s) offered and inspired did not include married life or sexual intimacy. Those who replaced these seemingly healthy church persons perhaps did not realize what they were in for, and the religious life and priesthood became places for sexually unhealthy people to hide. It has happened ever since. Most of the men with whom I was in the seminary were good people, but ill-prepared for priesthood. Many viewed priesthood as an easy job with a decent salary, great benefits, and instant status with the people they served. Priests have power, and they have to be careful how to use it. They are shown deference by parishioners, law enforcement officials, courts, business executives, and politicians. We saw an example of this deference when Pope Francis spoke before the Congress of the United States when he visited America in 2015.

I was hoping to spend my life in service to God and the faithful through religious life. Dysfunctional, immature, and dangerous sexual practices and policies drove me out. I was then hoping to spend my life in service to God and the faithful through the priesthood, but again dysfunctional, immature, and dangerous practices drove me out. The bottom line is that the Church will continue to implode unless and until it tackles the issues of sexuality and power. Currently, the fastest-growing religious group in America is that of former Catholics. The main reason: the clergy sexual abuse crisis. The vast majority of lay Catholics want priests to be able to marry and have families. The Vatican continues to ignore them. The same structures that created the clergy sexual abuse scandal are still in place, and children, teenagers, and vulnerable adults are at high risk of being sexually abused by clergy. The children being sexually abused today may not say anything about it for thirty or forty years, if ever, but be sure that sexual abuse by clergy continues unchecked.

PHOTOS

Robert M. Hoatson, Ph.D.

Childhood Home

*My Brother Bill; Me,
18 Months Old*

My Brothers, Ritchie and Billy, and Me

Kindergarten

4th Grade
Unaware of What was to Come

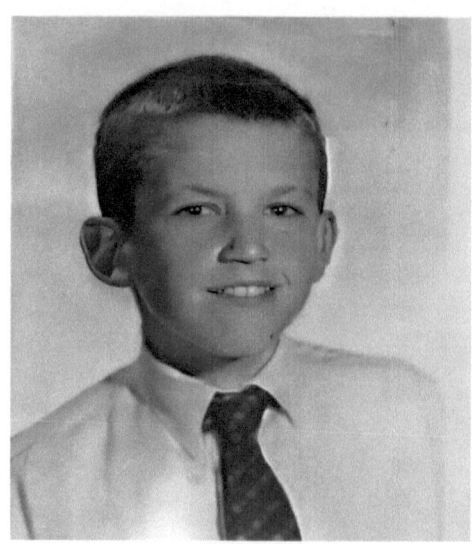

8th Grade Graduation
Me, Now Living with a Secret

About to Take My 1st Vows

*Singing at St. Joseph's,
Kingston, NY*

Celebrating with My Former Teachers

Me With My Mother and Father

Coaching JV Catholic Memorial, Boston

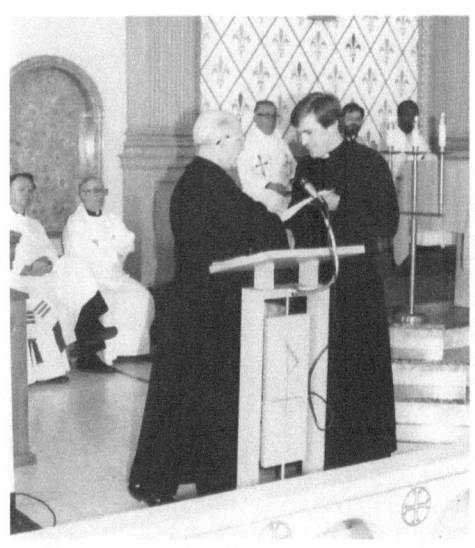

1980 Final Vows Irish Christian Brothers, My High School, Newark Essex Catholic High

Signing Final Vows Sheet

*My Entire Family Celebrates My
Final Vows
Essex Catholic High School*

Staff & Athletic Director Yearbook Photo, Blessed Sacrament High, New Rochelle, NY

1982 Chaplain, Catholic Memorial

Robert M. Hoatson, Ph.D.

*1988 Asst. Dean, School of
Education and Human Services,
St. John's University, NY*

*1990 Principal,
Sacred Heart High School,
Yonkers, NY*

*Me with Helen Nevin,
Associate Principal*

*Commencement Address
Sacred Heart,
Yonkers, NY*

Principal, Sacred Heart, Talking with Students

Cousin Marlene at Diaconate Ordination

Former Yonkers Principal Ordained Deacon in Newark

Robert M. Hoatson, a former teacher and administrator in five schools of the archdiocese, was ordained a transient deacon for the Archdiocese of Newark, N.J., on June 2 by Archbishop Theodore E. McCarrick of Newark at Our Lady of Mount Carmel Church in Ridgewood, N.J. He is expected to be ordained a priest next May.

Deacon Hoatson, 44, was an Irish Christian Brother from 1970 to 1996. He was principal of Sacred Heart School in Yonkers from 1992 to 1994 and Sacred Heart High School there from 1989 to 1994. Before that, he taught at St. Cecilia's School and Rice High School in Harlem, Blessed Sacrament High School in New Rochelle and Catholic Memorial High School in Boston.

He also served as assistant dean of the School of Education and Human Services at St. John's University in Queens. He received the university's Education for Justice Award in 1989.

Prior to entering Immaculate Conception Seminary at Seton Hall University in South Orange, N.J., in 1995, he served as assistant to the president of the William H. Sadlier Publishing Co. in Manhattan.

Deacon Hoatson, who was born in West Orange, N.J., received a bachelor's degree in English from Iona College, a master's in English from Manhattan College and a doctorate in educational administration and Church leadership from Fordham University.

He was a founding member of Catholic Urban Educators, a national network of Catholic inner-city school teachers and administrators. In 1990, he was named Educator of the Year by the Association of the Teachers of New York, and this past January received the National Catholic Educational Association's Outstanding Alumnus Award.

During the ordination, he was invested with the deacon's stole and chasuble by Father Philip F. Fabiano, O.F.M. Cap., former pastor of Sacred Heart parish in Yonkers. Deacon Hoatson will serve at St. Margaret of Cortona parish in Little Ferry, N.J.

Diaconate Ordination Procession, Our Lady of Mt. Carmel, Ridgewood, NJ

Preparing to Receive Diaconate Vestments

Family Diaconate Reception with Five Nieces & Nephews

1st Baptism at St. Margaret of Cortona, Little Ferry, NJ

*Televised Mass,
Archbishop McCarrick*

*May 24, 1997,
My Priestly Ordination*

My 1st Mass, Blessing with Water with Godson, Alex, St. Raphael's, Livingston, NJ

Me with the Pastor and a Seminarian

Robert M. Hoatson, Ph.D.

*Me with the Pastor and
Two Parishioners*

Greeting Parishioners After Mass

*Some Students From Holy Trinity
1998-2000*

*After Spanish Mass, Holy Trinity,
Hackensack, NJ*

*Farewell Party,
Holy Trinity,
Hackensack, NJ*

THE SACRIFICE OF THE MASSES

www.ingramcontent.com/pod-product-compliance
Lightning Source LLC
Chambersburg PA
CBHW020311010526
44107CB00001B/63